W9-BFE-389

wedding flowers

PHOTOGRAPHY BY CHRIS TUBBS

wedding flowers

paula pryke

RIZZOLI
NEW YORK

First published in the United States of America in 2004 by
Rizzoli International Publications, Inc.
300 Park Avenue South, New York, NY 10010
www.rizzoliusa.com

© **Jacqui Small** 2004
An imprint of Aurum Press Ltd,
25 Bedford Avenue, London WC1B 3AT, United Kingdom

All rights reserved. No part of this publication may be reproduced, stored in a retrieval system or transmitted in any form or by any means, electronic, mechanical or otherwise, without prior permission of the copyright holder

PUBLISHER Jacqui Small
ART DIRECTOR Valerie Fong
PHOTOGRAPHY Chris Tubbs
EDITORIAL MANAGER Vicki Vrint
PRODUCTION Geoff Barlow

ISBN–10: 0-8478-2581-7
ISBN–13: 978-0-8478-2581-3

Library of Congress Control Number: 2003104985

Third printing in 2005

2007 2006 2005 / 10 9 8 7 6 5 4 3

*For all the brides and grooms, and their loved
ones, who have let me be a part of their very
special day and who gave me the honor of
designing decorations for their weddings.*

PRINTED AND BOUND IN SINGAPORE

contents

the **role** of flowers

Flowers and foliage have been an integral part of wedding ceremonies around the world since time began. As tokens of love exchanged between men and women, they have a deep resonance in our romantic life and psyche. Flowers unite people and instantly serve as links between strangers, so they are vital to the heart of any wedding celebration. We all appreciate their aesthetic beauty, their perfect form, color, or heavenly fragrance but our ancestors appreciated them more for their meanings and their uses, and these still affect our choices today.

Flowers have featured in the beliefs, art, and medicine of our predecessors for thousands of years. They play a part in our myths and legends, and in religion and worship. They have become symbols of a whole range of human and spiritual experience and were originally chosen for this symbolism and for their fragrance, rather than their appearance or color. Greek brides carried marjoram to bring joy; Roman brides wove sprigs of rosemary into their headdresses to ensure devotion and love, and to make sure their marriages endured. Medieval brides wove together fresh garlands of flowers and herbs to wear on their heads, hoping that these would ward off evil spirits and bless their marriages with love, joy, good health, purity, fidelity, and fertility.

Many plants and flowers were given these symbolic meanings because of their nature or habitat. The box tree, for example, was thought to represent stoicism because it is evergreen and unaffected by the seasons. Lily-of-the-valley was considered an emblem of chastity and humility because of the bowed the bells and the pure white blooms. Today, brides may choose this delicate flower for its divine scent and the fabulous look of a posy of a mass of these lovely blooms.

floral traditions
The first wedding that really influenced the style of the modern ceremony was the marriage of Queen Victoria of England to Prince Albert—a great romance. Orange blossom was the flower of the day. It has a very long association with wedding nuptials. Juno, the Greek goddess of marriage, gave a wreath of orange blossom to Jupiter, her bridegroom, on their wedding night. In ancient times it signified fertility, but during the Victorian period it came to symbolize chastity and purity.

I suspect that the "orange blossom" that Queen Victoria wore was philadelphus (commonly known as orange blossom) unless blooms were gathered from orange trees in her estate greenhouses! Both flowers are extremely beautiful, as delicate as lace and as fragrant as the most precious bottle of perfume. Neither travels very easily though, so unless you are lucky enough to be marrying in an orange grove or in a garden filled with philadelphus, you may have to use vines of stephanotis or jasmine, or the sweet flowers of gardenias to add the fragrance. Scent is one of the ingredients of the perfect wedding that has endured the centuries. Fragrant herbs, foliage, and flowers help to create a unique floral perfume for your special day. For me the scent of 'Star Gazer' lilies and lily-of-the-valley will always bring back very happy memories of my wedding.

Queen Victoria's wedding also made the white wedding gown popular, and it became common for brides to hold a nosegay of concentric circles of all-white flowers, still known to this day in Britain as a "Victorian posy." As fashions changed and floristry techniques improved, cascading shower bouquets became popular. They were often very heavy as their mechanics were crude by today's standards.

Often the bride would give a flower from her bouquet to her bridesmaids, and occasionally bouquets were made of composite nosegays, so each bridesmaid could take flowers away. Sprigs of herbs and flowers were often pinned into the bodice of the bridal gown or attached to the gown itself. From the turn of the century, bridesmaids would also carry flowers—either huge wicker baskets filled with blooms or a floral staff. In more austere or religious circumstances a bible or prayer book was decorated with flowers and carried during the ceremony.

Historically, the main influence on wedding fashion has been economic. Not surprisingly when the world is enjoying peace and prosperity, lavish wedding style is in vogue. During the prosperous years of the twenties, some of our more elaborate fashion traditions came into effect. Wedding arches, candelabras and grand pedestals of flowers became the norm among the social elite, and the role of the wedding florist emerged. Later, brides in wartime Britain—and, to a lesser extnet the United States had to forgo many wedding traditions and wear simple dresses, often homemade and carry simple, wired, white nosegays of flowers usually fashioned into a cascade, crescent or a shower. Locally grown lilies, orchids, roses, and carnations were often mixed with fronds of asparagus ferns.

OPPOSITE A modern take on the traditional bridesmaid's basket. This zinc container is filled with summer flowers, including roses and sweet peas, and features garden fillers such as *Astrantia* and *Stachys byzantina*. Baskets such as this are suitable for younger bridesmaids.
ABOVE, CLOCKWISE FROM TOP The bridal party awaiting the arrival of the bride, holding classic nosegays of white sweet peas and lime green *Viburnum opulus*; A simple, traditional nosegay of lily-of-the-valley; A typical Victorian bouquet consisting of concentric circles of different varieties of flowers.

Ironically, the flower power period of the sixties saw little demand for extravagant flowers, and the trend for formal weddings almost disappeared as intimate weddings became popular. The wedding of Lady Diana Spencer to the Prince of Wales (heir to the British throne) in 1981, however, signaled a change from informal weddings to more traditional and lavish ceremonies. Diana's dress and cascading bouquet of intricately wired flowers marked a new trend for traditional shower bouquets, almost reminiscent of the twenties. The bouquet was nearly 4 feet (1.2 metres) long, and was filled with many scented flowers. Bouquets like this require a profusion of the best, most exquisite blooms and also much painstaking labor and are thus an expensive option.

choosing your flowers

For better or worse, for richer or poorer, fashions and trends are continually evolving and re-emerging, and choosing wedding flowers can be one of a bride's most daunting tasks. With modern farming techniques, you can have practically any flower your heart desires at almost any time of the year, and the choice of blooms is immense. There is an extraordinary repertoire of vibrant colors, intricate patterns, and alluring scents to choose from.

Beautiful weddings can be affordable on any budget; the key is to be realistic about what you can achieve. Start by deciding which flowers are essential, then move on to your "wish list." That way you can keep your needs and your desires in perspective—and spare your bridegroom

BELOW, CLOCKWISE FROM TOP This is a natural, round bouquet using mixed colors, suitable for a country wedding. It includes lilac *Rosa* 'Blue Gene' and *Rosa* 'Blue Curiosa', mixed with the white 'Avalanche' rose and the lime green blossom of *Viburnum opulus*; A classic summer bouquet of white peonies edged with hosta leaves. Round bouquets of a single variety suit any style of wedding gown; A contemporary and elegant over-arm bouquet of white calla lilies with green 'Midori' *Anthurium*. The shapes of these flowers perfectly suit this style of bouquet.

and father a shock! Often the cost of the flowers is split between both families—usually the bridegroom pays for the bridal bouquets and the decorations for the ceremony, and the bride (or her family) pays for the decorations for the wedding breakfast. Couples marrying much later in life often foot at least some, if not all, of the bill themselves. A sensible rule of thumb is to spend approximately the same on the flowers as you spend on your wedding dress.

In many cases your florist will be able to help you with a lot of the details, and once you have found someone you would like to work with, you can use them as a sounding board for your ideas. Often they will have arranged flowers in the same site or similar circumstances and will be able to give you lots of suggestions—and possibly show you pictures from their portfolio—to help you choose your look.

wedding styles

Broadly speaking, wedding flowers can be categorized as classic, romantic, or alternative in style; and the look you go for will probably be influenced by the location of the ceremony and reception. Classic flowers can be contemporary or historical and are by far the most popular choice among brides, as they suit most religious buildings and hotel receptions. The classic style is also the most economical to create, and by using the best of seasonal flowers and foliage, you are almost always guaranteed an elegant and opulent look.

The romantic look encompasses various styles, using scented and seasonal flowers in a soft and rustic way. Lots of delicate flowers may be massed together or arranged loosely. This feminine feel suits almost any site, but my personal favorite for this rural feel is, of course, a country wedding. Simply woven decorations including swags, garlands, and arches made from seasonal blooms, such as wheat, poppies, daisies, and herbs, are the essence of this style. The more decorations, the more draped ivies and candles, the better.

Alternative or innovative style involves a confident and striking theme, which can be minimalist. Usually a blank canvas such as a smart restaurant or a stylish all-white marquee is the best backdrop to display this kind of strong design, rather than a traditional hotel banqueting room. It suits unusual sites and urban weddings such as museums and art galleries (currently popular in Britain) and is often a more common choice for a second marriage. The innovative bride may choose to use deep colors (almost-black tulips and calla lilies) in a structured, architectural design or masses of one type of flower for all the decorations (pure white moth orchids, for example). Beware of this look if you are on a budget, as these single blooms are very expensive.

setting limitations
Brides tend to fall into one of two categories: those who have been planning their wedding since nursery and have a very firm idea of how they want their day to be and those who have never given it much thought and perhaps do not have time to worry about the details. If you have no idea about budget, you will need to use wedding books and magazines to get yourself up to speed. (These are also a useful source of contacts when gathering prices.) Regardless of the style of wedding you choose, it is advisable to determine what is affordable. It is not prudent to launch into a celebration that is going to lead you and your new husband into financial anxieties before the honeymoon is over.

If you are stretching the budget, there are a few things you could consider. Certain times of year are cheaper than others for weddings; most sites have a sliding scale of charges, with June being more expensive than January, for example. Some are less expensive if you choose a day other than Saturday or Sunday. Look for a site that will allow you to find your own caterer and provide your own wines and champagne. (Although you will have to pay corkage, you will still get better value.)

Keep the number of attendants down. The more bridesmaids, ushers, groomsmen, flower girls, and ring bearers you have, the grander the wedding becomes and the more outfits and presents have to be bought. Also think seriously about whom you want to invite—you may decide not to extend the invitations to someone's children or latest "date"!

For the decorations, choose a mass of seasonal flowers, and use plenty of berries and fruits in arrangements, as they are much less expensive than blooms. Failing that, go to a garden center, nursery, or farmers' market, and buy some lovely flowering houseplants, which, cleverly wrapped, will work as centerpieces. I have seen African violets, lavender, marguerites and chrysanthemums work well when presented in this way.

Look for inexpensive votives, which will add ambiance to the table. (You will also be able to re-use these at future parties.) Groups of candles work well for an evening function, just edge in ivy and assorted greenery or float one or two flower heads with some floating candles in bowls. For a winter wedding, candles in mounds of shelled nuts with perhaps a tangerine is also very effective. Another option is to use a bowl of colorful fruit, arranged well. (Your caterer should be able to

ABOVE The choice of a strong color for the bridal gown demands flowers that are of the same intensity as the fabric of the dress. The red 'Grand Prix' roses and Singapore orchids perfectly complement the gown, while the lime-green cymbidium orchids and the green *Amaranthus* make a striking contrast. The trailing shower bouquet balances the full skirt of the gown beautifully.

rent some footed glass bowls for you.) That way your guests can pick too! Another inexpensive and easy option that can be most effective is to float one or two flower heads along with floating candles in a pretty bowl on each table. Whatever you do, don't stint on hiring your photographer, as he or she will provide your reminder of the special day. Take great care in choosing this trusted professional. Whatever ceremony you choose—and however you decide to decorate it—remember that all brides look fantastic on the day and every wedding has its own unique moments and beauty.

BELOW, LEFT TO RIGHT The bride and groom enjoy a moment together—it's important to savor the day, as it passes so quickly.

themes

One of the drawbacks to planning a wedding is that there are so many ways you can personalize your special day. Although this proliferation of choices can be quite liberating, it can also make you a slave to your wedding day so beware! A theme can be a lovely idea, but when you find yourself locked into the Internet looking for an obscure variety of favors or peppermint-colored ostrich feathers, be easy on yourself! Remember, throughout the planning, your aesthetic should be to create an original, striking, and coordinated theme, which lends dignity, beauty, and joy to even the smallest of weddings.

I have had the pleasure of arranging flowers for a range of themes—from *A Midsummer Night's Dream* and *Swan Lake* to Winnie the Pooh. Royal figures such as Princess Grace and Princess Margaret have influenced weddings, as have Hollywood movies *Moulin Rouge* and *Gone with the Wind*. Whatever you choose, flowers can complement your theme—a pony and trap can be decked out with buckets of wild blooms, or a much-loved sports car or vintage vehicle can be trimmed with flowers.

inspiration

Sometimes the inspiration for a theme can come from the most unlikely places. One bride used lilac feathers for her invitations, which started a very strong color theme. In the end, the wedding was enhanced by lavender-scented candles, bowls of lilac candies, masses of lilac roses (including 'Blue Curiosa' and 'Sterling Silver'), and other lilac summer flowers, including ageratum, sweet peas, and lisianthus. Each guest was presented with a lilac box containing delicious violet creams, topped with a crystallized violet. One very beautiful—but staggeringly expensive—theme used gardenia blooms by the thousand to create one of the most fragrant weddings I have every witnessed.

Another bride used citrus fruits as a theme, taking her husband's business (importing these fruits) as inspiration. The celebrations started with citrus cocktails. The tables were decorated with small kumquats in vases topped with orange Iceland poppies and mounds of orange ranunculus. The top table was garlanded with bunches of greenbriar and kumquats, and trimmed with florets of stephanotis. For the larger arrangements, topiary pyramids of citrus fruits were created with a few stephanotis florets and lime leaves. Large vases were lined with large orange slices and filled with long-stemmed, orange "French" tulips. The hors d'oeuvres included a salad with pink grapefruit, and, of course, the cake was trimmed with kumquats and candied oranges. Each guest's place was marked with a jar of homemade marmalade for them to take home.

For my own wedding, I used the theme of harvest, which appealed to me as I was brought up in arable farming country. Wheat featured on the invitations, the place cards, and, of course, in the decorations. Although it's not my favorite flower, it set the perfect tone for my late summer wedding. Sunflowers are also a popular choice for late-summer weddings, and at one I attended, the place cards were printed on packets of sunflower seeds for the guests to take away and plant as a memento the following year.

Wines and vines are a popular theme, with many marriages taking place in vineyards or with a love of wine acting as inspiration for a theme for the tables. For one vineyard wedding I attended, candelabras were covered in old vines and then swathed with young green grapes and clusters of 'Black Baccara' roses, the color of a perfect bordeaux wine.

Another bride chose a favorite Henry David Thoreau quote, "Go confidently in the direction of your dreams," and had a calligrapher write it around the middle of the dining tables in lavender ink. She filled the center of the table with lavender and sweet-pea arrangements encircled by masses of votive lights (30 per table) to beautiful effect.

Countries can also provide inspiration — perhaps a favorite vacation spot, or the location of the proposal. The Provençal region of France, with its olive trees, geraniums, sunflowers, and lavender, works well, as does Spanish style, with masses of oleander, bougainvilleas, and a really bright theme. Moroccan style is another very popular choice, and we have themed many weddings around the feel of the sunny climate of North Africa and its tradition for decorating with bright colors.

wedding traditions
Whatever your theme and choice of flowers, you will probably want to include the time-honored tradition of old, new, borrowed, and blue. The "old" symbolizes your previous life and ties with your family (a piece of jewelry is often used for this). Something new symbolizes the journey into your new life, and this is always easy to achieve. A new perfume for your wedding will always remind you of the day. Traditionally, borrowing something from a happily married couple will bring you the same good fortune. Brides often borrow their veil or a lace handkerchief or garter. And, finally, blue has long been associated with devotion and loyalty and is thought to ward off evil spirits. Often a little blue bow is sewn into the bridal gown, or occasionally blue flowers are entwined into the bridal bouquet.

ABOVE, CLOCKWISE FROM TOP When planning arrangements for the site, note that two large arrangements have more impact than several smaller ones. The bronze sculpture is perfect for decorating with flowers, as it is above eye level. A carpet of rose petals and rose chairbacks make a fragrant aisle for the bride and groom; The bride chose to carry her favorite flowers (purple sweet peas) and the color was picked up in larger arrangements, as well as on the tables; Massed flower heads and candles in a clear plastic container create a patchwork of flowers which is simple (if expensive) to recreate.

working with a florist
Like most things in life, the best way to find a florist is by personal recommendation; but wedding magazines can also be a useful source. Make an appointment

to visit your florist, so that you have time to sit down and look through their portfolio. A face-to-face meeting is important, because it gives the designer a chance to get a full image of you and your personality, as well as your height and plans for the day. Professional designers are capable of working in many different styles, and it is their role to create a sense of your own personal preference in your floral design. The designer should not dictate a style, but should work with you to create it.

If you are uncertain about what you want, your florist should help you develop a plan you are happy with. This will take place over a series of meetings—very rarely is everything decided on the first day—so do not worry if you have not achieved a grand plan at your first meeting. Do give the designer your budget and ask her whether it is realistic. A real professional can help you focus on the important elements, rather than on anything impractical you may have on your list.

BELOW, CLOCKWISE FROM TOP An iron arch over a gate provides the perfect floral welcome for the wedding party when decorated with flowers, including trailing moth orchids, bowers of white bougainvillea, and fronds of *Amaranthus*. A preliminary visit with your florist will enable you to make the most of existing features at the venue, such as this archway; Garden roses and lady's mantle in a round glass vase suit this chic city wedding with a white-and-green theme; This three-tiered wedding cake has been decorated simply with delicate, scented florets of tuberose.

It is useful for the florist if you make your first appointment once you have chosen your site and dress. Without this information, you may find it difficult to discuss any of the details. Many brides take along images of the kind of flowers they like or even the style of arrangement they are looking for. It is also helpful to take information on your bridesmaids and flower girls, including dress color and a swatch of fabric, as well as information on the ceremony and a floor plan of the reception.

Your florist should be able to outline a costing for you; once confirmed, it is a good idea to meet them at the site, to go through all the details. You can also discuss tablecloths, napkins, candles, and any other aspects of the decoration. Check that your final quote includes everything you requested and that the delivery addresses and times will suit your schedule.

If you employ a professional, it is up to them to make sure that all your flowers are delivered and presented to you in their best condition. Bear in mind that for an opulent look, your florist will be aiming to get your flowers into full bloom and will not be presenting them to you in the freshest and most closed form which, you might choose if you were purchasing flowers for your home.

planning ahead It takes at least six
months to plan a formal wedding on a large scale, but it is easy to arrange a less formal celebration in three

months or less. Also, if you pick a popular time of the year, you will find that many sites and services get booked up ahead of time, and you may have to be flexible about your date. When it comes to the flowers, you can have most varieties at most times of the year, but unless you are the daughter of a millionaire (or are marrying one!) do not plan to have lily-of-the-valley on every table outside the month of May. If sweet peas are your chosen flower, it obviously makes sense to hold your wedding during the summer months rather than the depths of winter.

Generally speaking, although I am happy to source flowers out of season for any of my brides, in my experience seasonal flowers tend to look more effective. Nature is a great mentor, and following the trends of the season will give the most harmonious and beautiful results. The other major consideration is that certain dates are peak times for the flower industry. If you are a real romantic and decide to get married on Valentine's Day, it may be difficult to get a florist to commit to arranging your wedding flowers, and you will certainly spend more on them.

arranging your own flowers
If you decide to arrange some of your own flowers, it is advisable to have a professional take care of your bridal bouquet and all the large assemblies or intricate, complicated designs. You will then have peace of mind that your own bouquet will look great, the flowers for the photographs will be beautiful, and any large arrangements will be safely constructed.

It is important to be realistic about what you can achieve in the time you have. Even if you are planning a small and intimate wedding, enlist the help of some friends or family and have a clear plan of action. Very few florists work alone, and you will find that, for an amateur, each arrangement will take a long time to perfect. Make a list of all the arrangements you wish to create and the components for each one, including sundries such as floral foam and tape. It is helpful to have someone to help you lift and carry, because flower arranging is back breaking work. Whatever you plan, work out a schedule that includes conditioning the flowers, as this can take half a day! They will need a long drink of tepid water to revive them (as they may have been in transit for a while), and the stems should be cut diagonally with secateurs, scissors, or a knife to take up the water. It is a good idea to use flower food mixed in with the water, as this improves their condition. It is also imperative to clean all your buckets first (I often use bleach), so that bacteria don't contaminate the water. Add enough water to fill the buckets and leave them for at least five hours or overnight, so that everything is fresh and strong when you begin to arrange your flowers.

When you have completed the arrangements, add water mixed with flower food. You can also spray water with a spray bottle—this will enhance the life of the flowers, but don't overdo it or use this method with orchids, which can mark.

The best weddings I have seen have one special formula: the bride and groom are hopelessly in love and in tune with the celebrations planned and are sharing their love with their family and friends. It is important to plan your day carefully, of course, but do not allow yourself to become obsessed with the details, as this only leads to stress. On the day, just enjoy yourself—it will seem like the fastest day you have ever lived and will almost be over before it has started, so savor every wonderful minute of it.

Whichever floral decorations you choose and however you achieve your wedding design, your flowers will be central to the event and will symbolize the hope, love and joy of your wedding celebrations.

ABOVE A marquee is a blank canvas which is perfectly suited to decoration with bright-colored flowers. Tall taper candles and candelabras make the most of the space and create canopies of color above the heads of the diners. Chairs, seat pads, and linen can be rented to complement your theme and will create a smart coordinated look.

working with nature

Whatever date you choose for your wedding, seasonal flowers are by far the best option. What is the point of purchasing expensive, imported blossoms in fall when gardens are full of jewel-like petals and flame-colored foliage is in abundance, or in spring when nature rejoices in whites and soft colours? Our natural desires are in tune with the seasons, so look around you for inspiration. Go for a long country walk, see what is available at your local farmers' market, and go to specialist flower shops to look for the seasonal blooms.

Once I imported peonies from Australia for a November wedding in England. The long journey from the other side of the world and the lack of other seasonal flowers to accompany the blooms detracted from the natural, indescribable beauty of peonies used in season. This is partly because our perception and enjoyment of certain types of flowers (and foods) is influenced

by the seasons. In spring we enjoy the pastel blooms of the early part of the year while summer brings masses of color. As the nights draw in and the temperature drops, we yearn for the warm reds and oranges of fall, and in winter we look for whites, mossy green branches and deep red berries.

spring In spring a mass of seasonal color is available, thanks to the hybridization of one particular flower—the tulip. You can buy commercially grown tulips in over 500 varieties, from pure white to marbled red and yellow, and the deepest black. They are an extremely versatile flower and can be made to look wild and rustic, romantic and pretty, or stylized and modern, and so they suit any interior. The taller and more elegant varieties are known as "French" tulips. My favorite spring flowers, however, are ranunculus. They are so beautiful, and are available in many colors from greenish white to dark burgundy and even chocolate brown. Ranunculus also come in very deep and brightly colored varieties. They make fantastic flowers for bouquets and work very well in arrangements and in wired work.

For scent in spring, there are many possibilities, from fragrant jasmine vines to heady hyacinths. 'Paper White' narcissi, freesias, and mimosa are also very fragrant, and some early blossom branches have a light scent, too. Huge glass vases of pink cherry blossom look great arranged en masse. If you fancy a vibrant yellow theme, with daffodils and tulips, you can add scent by using vases of the spherical blossoms of mimosa. For larger displays, tall branches of forsythia work well, and yellow lilies can be found in spring and throughout the year. For deep color anemones could be your spring choice. These elegant flowers are available in deep purple and lavender, as well as bright red and deep pink. They suit both bouquets and centerpieces, and can be very eyecatching arranged simply, en masse. Anemones also look great bunched beneath the head to create a living tree topiary.

Other special spring flowers include grape hyacinths in blue and white, hellebores in a range of colors, and the very charming checker lily. These delicate flowers make fabulous nosegays and charming romantic arrangements for tables. Violets are also at their best in the spring, and although very delicate and short-lived, are often associated with Valentine's Day and true love. Parma violets, from Italy, usually come wrapped in leaves and bound with raffia to keep the stems as straight as possible and so look just perfect massed together with these leaves edging them. Early pussy-willow branches and (in mild climates) the sweetly scented blossom of the winter-flowering viburnums are ideal for brightening up flower arrangements and bouquets in the earlier part of the year.

early summer
In late spring and early summer, the most popular time of year for weddings, there is an abundance of floral material available. I am very drawn to the pale pinks and blues of this time of the year. I love blowsy peonies and scented garden roses for round bouquets, mixed with lily-of-the-valley or aromatic lavender. Trails of honeysuckle and spray roses are just divine for longer, wilder natural bouquets. Choose stately foxgloves, sweet-scented stocks, and huge hybrid delphiniums, spiked with star-shaped musky lilies for large arrangements, with long branches of foliage.

If these flowers are all too blowsy, and you prefer a pared-down summer theme pick a single flower for your inspiration, such as the humble daisy or cornflower. I have seen many weddings using these two blooms, and I have to say that the simplicity of a bunch of daisies in a nosegay or in simple pitchers on the table

is quite breathtaking. Cornflowers also work well—arranged en masse, floating in a bowl, or in a simple bunch with grasses and marguerites and a few summer thistles such as *Eryngium* or *Echinops*.

Lavender is a favorite scented summer flower. It has inspired many of my designs. It looks good in bouquets, tied onto baskets for bridesmaids to carry, or encircling arrangements. If you grow lavender a few stems tied onto each napkin are a great way of spreading its wonderful scent and they make a lovely keepsake for your guests.

The new leaf growth of large deciduous trees (including *Sorbus* and beech) is very lush at this time of year. Great summer ground foliage includes hosta leaves and the arched stems of Solomon's seal, whose bright green hues set off mixed, rich-colored centerpieces beautifully.

OPPOSITE If you have set your heart on scented garden roses, the best months to marry are between June and September, when they are at their best and most plentiful.
ABOVE, CLOCKWISE FROM TOP LEFT Here, 'Bianca Candy' roses and eustoma have been made to look more summery by using 'Pink Pearl' snowberries; An alternative to wearing a corsage is to pin floral decorations onto your accessories. For this winter wedding, slipper orchids have been chosen to complement a green bag; Summer is the best time for your wedding if you want to use lilacs and blue flowers, as there is such a wide range of blossoms to choose from, including sweet peas, hydrangeas, and scabious.

late summer

The late summer months bring a wealth of striking, bright-colored flowers such as dahlias, achilleas, sunflowers, and zinnias. These all suit simple displays or topiary arrangements, where their large heads make a patchwork of color. Fabulous seed heads include the puffy, pointed pods of *Physalis* and the seed heads of poppies and scabious. The plump berries from viburnum and spiky blackberries from country lanes make for mouth-watering sumptuous arrangements.

Spongy celosia is another gorgeous flower available in an array of vibrant colors. Lilies can be found all year but it is in summer that you get some of the more traditional varieties (such as 'Regalia') and the best scents. One lovely modern hybrid is 'Barbaresco', which is a deep pink color and has the most delicious fragrance when fully opened. Old-fashioned snapdragons are also abundant and can be found in any color to suit your theme from bright pink to acid yellow. Cosmos also flower late and are perfect if you like a wild or understated look. The chocolate-scented *Cosmos atrosanguineus* is available during August and September. Pink and white cosmos can be found in late summer.

Hydrangeas are strong now, too. You can cut the florets up and include them in your headdresses. Whole flower heads look fabulous in large decorations or en masse.

fall

Autumn brings rich color schemes as foliage begins to display fabulous fall colors. Gladioli and chrysanthemums are in season, and the slender-stemmed nerines (from perfect white and pink through to bright red) are the new jewels of the season. Massed together, they make stunning round nosegays or great living topiary trees. Mix the blood red ones with purple *Callicarpa* berries, brown *Hypericum* berries and some seasonal foliage, and add just one or two branches of crab apples for a sumptuous autumnal arrangement. The trailing stems of love-lies-bleeding are also fabulous at this time and, used with hydrangeas and fall foliage, can make easy work of creating large arches or decorating huppahs.

There are also still some great lime greens, including the elegant twisted spires of bells of Ireland. The spider chrysanthemum 'Shamrock' is great for large displays, while the smaller santini chrysanthemum 'Kermit' is great for centerpieces and small groupings. The green zinnia 'Envy', the lime-green-berried *Hypericum* 'Jade Flair', and the final stems of *Alchemilla mollis* add a bright tinge of green, which makes any color look fresher and more vibrant. For a blue theme in fall use hydrangeas, delphiniums, or thistles. For lilac, you may get some alliums and the lilac roses 'Blue Curiosa' and 'Sterling Silver', while gladioli, lisianthus, and *Trachelium* are all available in a range of lilac and purple hues.

For me, though, a fall wedding is the best opportunity to make use of the fruit that is abundant and inexpensive at this time of year. It is an excellent time to take a harvest theme and use wheat, barley, hops, vines, and other staples in your decorations. Apple topiaries or baskets filled with flowers look mouth watering, or you can fill glass vases with tiny crab apples and top with a mixed seasonal hand-tie for a loose, country effect.

If you are looking for autumn scent use late-flowering garden roses or herbs. I love angelica and the fragrant fronds of dill. Flowering mint and marjoram also add scent and color to fall centrepieces. Herbs are not only an effective addition to bouquets and table-top arrangements, they can be woven into garlands or even scattered on the floor of the venue.

ABOVE Daisies are a classic choice for a country wedding. The chrysanthemums used here (*Chrysanthemum* 'Reagan White') are available all year round. They are arranged in a terracotta pot with a rope handle, which makes this an easy display for a young bridesmaid to carry, and put down when necessary.

BELOW, CLOCKWISE FROM TOP RIGHT
Late summer- or autumn-flowering chocolate cosmos are an unusual, but striking, bridal flower, as they are quite difficult to acquire; Fruit and vegetables can be used at any time of year to add color and texture to your flower arrangements. Here, a savoy cabbage is filled with 'Iceberg' roses for a simple centrepiece; Red and orange flowers are more popular in the fall and winter months. Here red nerines are mixed with open roses, pincushion proteas, berries, and rosehips to create a spectacular and colourful candelabra.

winter

Wintertime brings a new range of flowers for the bride to use. Rich colors appeal to our senses and traditional rich fare is fuel for our bodies. One winter special is *Euphorbia fulgens*, which is an arched stem of many tiny florets. It is related to poinsettias and oozes a milky sap, which can be an irritant to your skin, so be careful when using it or wear protective gloves. These delicate flowers are great in vase arrangements and pedestals as they give a lovely trail to the overall shape. Cymbidium orchids are at their best in the winter months and the large varieties work well in huge pedestal arrangements. The florets make great corsages for wrists or handbags, and the mini cymbidiums are ideal for wiring into headdresses. Cymbidium orchids are very long-lasting and versatile. They last well out of water, and so the flower heads can be scattered on a table with votives or wired into twiggy wreathes to add color. Their range of color is immense, and the new burgundy and brown varieties are most intriguing. A personal favorite of mine is lime green with burgundy blooms, and I love to mix this with deep 'Black Baccara' roses and interesting foliage for a striking effect.

Of course, a winter wedding is all about using the rich evergreen foliage, such as ivy, mistletoe, and spruce, which has always held a special significance for us because of its association with fidelity and fertility. These plants are very aromatic, and the use of spruce and eucalyptus in your wedding decorations will also give the ceremony a very fresh and clean scent as well as a seasonal look.

In some zones, spring flowers also start to come back on the scene, and so tulips, ranunculus, anemones, and hyacinths are available again. Amaryllis are an option now too and these look stunning in large arrangements and also cut up as table decorations. If you use them in pots they work well lined up on mantelpieces and in church windows, surrounded by a mass of votives and other candles. One of my favorite festive arrangements with amaryllis uses it bunched as a topiary tree set on a flat dish, and anchored by a pinholder frog or packed into low pots filled with floral foam.

There are also some fantastic berries and seed heads on offer in winter, and one of my favourites is skimmia—both in its berried form and used as flowering stems. Eucalyptus is great too, and the gray seed heads add a touch of festive silver to any bunch. Holly berries in red and yellow also add a splash of bright color to large groupings of flowers. Alternatively, of course, roses are still very much available and are an excellent source of rich color. In winter, they are often used in red or white arrangements, to great effect, along with gerberas and chrysanthemums, which are available all the year round.

spring wedding

planning a wedding takes a lot of organization, and the process was even more complicated for Monica and John, who were living and working in Asia and marrying in England. They were making arrangements from a long distance and in a different time zone. After a few frantic visits back home to get things under way, they decided to appoint a wedding planner, Sophie Lillingstone, to advise them and take care of all arrangements for the day, which gave them peace of mind to enjoy their wedding.

Beacuse their ceremony took place in spring, we were able to use fresh growth from deciduous trees (including mountain ash and beech) in the decorations. We combined this with masses of fresh fragrant herbs, mixed with peonies, the first garden roses, and sweet peas. For the ceremony, Monica chose a white-and-cream color scheme to stand out in the grand marble interior of the church and to match the bridal-party flowers. She decided on stephanotis florets as boutonnieres for the bridegroom and his groomsmen, and her attendants also wore this flower. The three adult bridesmaids wore it in their headdresses, while the three flower girls had stephanotis florets incorporated into their decorations. They also held beautifully scented nosegays of sweet peas and *Viburnum opulus*. For her own bouquet, Monica chose to carry a beautiful nosegay of white peonies edged with hosta leaves.

For their reception, they chose to use more vibrant blues and pinks to soften the interior of the site and fill it with scent. For the entrance we created an arch by placing two pedestals on either side of a corridor and using long branches of foliage to meet in the middle. Because the ballroom was on the second floor, garlands of ivy and roses were arranged all the way along the bannisters to invite the guests upstairs. Mantelpieces are perfect for floral decorations, as they are exactly the right height to brighten the room. We decorated one with a formal front-facing arrangement and another with lots of round pots of rosemary, filled with roses, sweet peas, and masses of twinkling votive lights. Rosemary became a dominant theme for the table arrangements, and we used a mixture of high and low displays. Since the tables were only 2 feet (60 cm) across, we chose tall fluted vases and filled these with rosemary, topped with herbs, roses, and peonies with a collar of ivy. The low-level arrangements were created by covering glass tumblers with rosemary and hand-tying small posies of butterfly lavender, astrantia, roses, and sweet peas. Pillar candles were encircled with rosemary, and each guest had a small nosegay of thyme, mint, lavender, and rosemary tied with raffia on their napkin.

ABOVE White peonies are readily available for about six weeks in the middle of the year and are the quintessential bouquet flower. The bridegroom and the groomsmen all wore scented florets of stephanotis for their boutonnieres. **LEFT** Monica chose to use white and green for the church and her bridal flowers. This is quite a traditional choice and often most complementary for dark church interiors. The bridesmaids and flower girls are clutching bouquets of white sweet peas mixed with *Viburnum opulus*.

ABOVE LEFT The white theme is picked up in the classic cars, which have been decorated with ribbons. **ABOVE RIGHT** A simple hand-tied bouquet of *Viburnum opulus* and white sweet peas, to be carried by one of the bridesmaids. It's advisable to put bouquets like this in water during the reception to prevent them from drooping. **LEFT** Heavy marble interiors found in many religious buildings suit grand arrangements. White and cream often show up best, being more noticeable than mixed colors or dark shades, such as blue, purple, and burgundy. This arrangement includes spring branches mixed with delphiniums, stocks and lilies.

"It is the art of a great florist to decorate a space and create an atmosphere that is a true reflection of the couple. Paula achieved this to perfection—they were over the moon!" SOPHIE

ABOVE LEFT White peonies are here edged with seasonal hosta leaves. If you are choosing white wedding flowers and wearing an ivory gown, an edging of leaves separates the flowers from the color of the fabric. **ABOVE** Two pedestals are placed on either side of a corridor to create the effect of an arch. The tall branches of white-leaf foliage have been used asymmetrically and joined in the center. Grand arrangements such as these are best created *in situ,* so that the flowers are designed to fit the space. Blue 'Harlequin' delphiniums give height to the arrangement, while the lilies (*Lilium* 'Sissi') create a welcoming scent. **LEFT** The mantelpiece is the perfect place for a contrasting display. **OPPOSITE (CLOCKWISE FROM TOP LEFT)** Occasional-table arrangements, featuring cut rosemary around a glass tumbler, are filled with a rose-and-herb nosegay; Tall glass vases filled with rosemary are topped with a nosegay of hand-tied roses and herbs; Each napkin is decorated with herbs tied with raffia; A stair-case garland marks the route for the guests.

summer wedding

an informal, country wedding

is the ideal occasion for romantic summer flowers. Julie's marriage to
Fred is a perfect example. The wedding was held at a local church, with
the reception in a huge marquee on the family's farm. As soon as Julie
and Fred announced their engagement, Julie's father and brother started
work leveling out part of a field and re-sowing the grass so that they
could pitch a marquee overlooking the picturesque valley where Julie
had grown up. It was no coincidence that Julie, who manages a farm
office, picked late summer for her wedding, once the harvest was over.
Since she is passionate about flowers, we knew that she would want to
include lots of floral arrangements in her wedding scheme. She chose to
incorporate some of the wildflowers grown on her farm, such as rushes
and hops, as well as some cultivated wheat in her arrangements. Country
weddings suit color, and as Julie had chosen lilac for her bridesmaids'
dresses, a blue-and-lilac theme soon started to emerge.

It was a real rural affair: many of the villagers came to see Julie at the church, and the couple rode their horses from the church
to the reception. Julie practiced riding sidesaddle with a blanket to see if she could cope with her bridal gown, and on the day the
couple made this romantic trip together with friends and family following on foot for the short journey from church to marquee.

Julie cut some long vines of hops, which we bound with wire. We added bunches of wheat and then open, white lilies and bright
blue hydrangea heads. Arches can be difficult to construct since there are often no fixings in the walls to anchor the greenery and
flowers. Julie's church benefited by having a central light to which we could attach the wire, and there were also some metal fixtures
around the edge of the door which we were able to use. It is important to check what is allowed in the venue when you are planning
your ceremony, before deciding on any decorations that may not be practical or permitted.

We lined the aisle with metal candelabras, containing thick round candles, and round rings of flowers in a blue-and-white
theme using lilies, hydrangeas, and roses, along with lots of trailing ivies. Two large terracotta amphoras were set at the top of the
aisle, on either side of the altar, and a huge spray of flowers was arranged along the altar. To set the scene, votives were lit in all the
church windows, and trailing flower arrangements were placed on any available windowsill.

OPPOSITE Julie and Fred pose for photographs beneath the floral arch, which was created using hops bound together, with sheaves of wheat tied on. We added hydrangea heads and open 'Casa Blanca' lilies. BELOW When the pews are not suitable for pew-end arrangements, or when you wish to add candlelight, free-standing candelabras lining the pews are a nice idea. These chunky candelabras were created using a small floral foam wreath frame placed on top of the candelabra and filled with hydrangeas, lilies, and roses. RIGHT The choice of colors for the flowers for Julie's wedding was inspired the fabric for the bridesmaids' dresses—a popular source of inspiration for a theme.

LEFT It's customary to have two arrangements flanking the altar. Here terracotta amphoras have been chosen to give an informal feel. The choice of container is important in creating the right overall look. **ABOVE** White rose boutonnieres are edged with sea holly and dark green ivy leaves. **BELOW, LEFT** One of Julie's bridesmaids, carrying her floral bag. **BELOW, RIGHT** Julie's bridal bouquet is a lovely mixture of 'Blue Curiosa', 'Blue Gene', and 'Avalanche' (white) roses with smaller, lilac 'Sterling Silver' roses. The spheres of *Viburnum opulus* add a hint of lime and make the bouquet more vibrant in color.

"When I walked into the church I was completely overwhelmed by how it had been transformed in such a short time. The flowers in the marquee were fantastic too!" JULIE

TOP LEFT The happy bridal party line up for the family photos outside the church. The bridesmaids' hair and bouquets are trimmed with the same coordinating organza ribbon. **TOP RIGHT** One of the bridesmaids' bags filled with 'Blue Curiosa' roses. The roses are hand-tied and then placed in water-filled plastic bags. **LEFT** The Lady Chapel decked with vases, candles, and trailing window arrangements surrounded by many votives.

FAR LEFT, TOP Sprays of fragrant stephanotis and masses of rose petals and frosted votive lights add the finishing touch to the cake. OPPOSITE, TOP RIGHT Julie's bridesmaids run across from the field from the marquee to her home, through a path of mushroom baskets filled with hydrangeas and roses. FAR LEFT Classic candelabras always look elegant at a reception. Usually we arrange flowers at the top and in a ring at the base, allowing the guests to see across the table. LEFT The candelabras spill with seasonal blue flowers—cornflowers, *Veronica*, garden roses, sweet peas, and hydrangeas. Urns of blue hydrangea and ivy are also used to decorate the huge marquee. ABOVE The bridesmaids' bouquets are smaller versions of Julie's bouquet, with sweet peas as well roses. RIGHT Mushroom baskets are a lovely way to mark out a patch in a beautiful rural setting like this. The baskets have been lined with plastic and filled with floral foam and flowers.

fall wedding

rich, warm colors are perfect for a fall wedding—and Bella and Nick used just such a theme for their special day. They chose to celebrate it at two alternative sites. As they wanted to involve their treasured dog in the ceremony, they needed to find two locations that were fairly relaxed about this. Bella had often attended lectures at The Royal Geographical Society and discovered that, having their own dog in permanent residence, they were happy to allow Pip to act as bridesmaid for the civil ceremony. The wedding party traveled to the reception in an old-style double-decker London bus and, to fuel the celebrations, the conductors handed each guest a hand-embroidered bag filled with bottles of chilled champagne and smoked almonds. For their reception, Nick and Bella chose an historic period property that has retained most of its original features and has been lovingly restored by its owners, who often rent it out to television companies as a setting for period dramas.

Bella is a discerning flower lover who had recently edited a book on herbs, so together we made an early-morning trip to a local flower market where we decided that the floral arrangements would have a fragrant herbal theme throughout. Bella also decided to make the most of the early autumnal blooms and foliage, and she wanted the overall effect to include native plants. She decided her romantic dress would perfectly suit a round bouquet of chocolate cosmos, and I kept my fingers crossed, hoping there would be some available for her. They are available in scant quantities from late summer, and I feared that October would be too late. The fragile beauty of their stems and the fact they smell divinely of rich chocolate add to their attraction. We settled on an alternative of late garden roses, in case cosmos did prove to be unavailable. (If you set your heart on a particular flower, especially an uncommon one, it is a good idea to have an alternative in mind to avoid disappointment.)

At the reception, aromatic herbs, including myrtle, were woven into garlands and hung on the staircases. Loosely arranged herbs, such as dill, and garden roses were placed in simple earthernware jugs. Bella had also picked huge quantities of lavender and rosemary from her mother's country garden, and every old oak floor in the house was strewn with them, so that as the guests moved around the house, the herbs released their familiar fragrance. Hop vines garlanded the bar table and were twisted around pillars in the main reception room, while pitchers of feverfew daisies decorated the trestle tables.

"As we stepped inside the house on that cool October evening, the room was filled with the welcoming aroma of herbs and old-fashioned roses. It was everything that we dreamed it would be." BELLA

OPPOSITE Bella sits with her delicious bouquet of chocolate cosmos. The deep velvet texture of cosmos and the delectable color (not quite brown and not quite burgundy) make these flowers a real treasure. **LEFT** Bella wore a romantic flounced dress decorated with roses, which are one of her favorite flowers and were part of the theme throughout the celebration. **ABOVE** The elegant Pip in the silk ruff that Bella had made by jewelry designer Heidi Sturgess. **BELOW, LEFT AND RIGHT** Breaking with convention, Bella and Nick leave for the ceremony together in a plum-colored Karma Cab. The bumpers are decorated with brightly colored *faux* flowers and the interior echoes the exotic theme. Both complement the flowers on Bella's dress.

RIGHT This herb garland is made from bay, rosemary, sage, and thyme, with a touch of scented eucalyptus, trailing ivy, and sea holly thistle. The foliage is bound onto a rope using a heavy blue spool wire. The garland is secured to the handrail of the staircase with string. **BELOW** Galvanized buckets of herbs and old-fashioned roses, loosely arranged, are a feature in every room of the house. **BELOW RIGHT** Earthenware pots are filled with 'Black Baccara' and 'Xtreme' roses, flowering mint, dill, and ivy, to great effect.

ABOVE Bella and Nick share a moment together after the ceremony. They brought back dried rose petals from a trip to Morocco and scattered these at the site. Baskets of petals were also offered to the guests to throw as confetti as they left the building. **TOP RIGHT** An earthenware pot containing scented roses, sage, dill, rosemary, and mint welcomes the guests at the front door. **RIGHT** For this historic home, antique galvanized buckets and earthenware pots are perfect for the floral arrangements. They suit the interior and match Bella and Nick's vision for the day.

winter wedding

a cozy and warm winter wedding

brought together Jane's English family with Ewan's clan from Scotland. Traditional Scottish wedding dress and Scottish dancing gave the wedding a flavor of the north, while their choice of sites gave it a sophisticated urban feel. (Jane and Ewan chose to hold their ceremony in a Catholic church in the city center, and decided on a nearby club for the reception.)

For the church decorations Jane worked with the church florist to create large arrangements in her chosen scheme of bright red and lime green. Rich green foliage is perfect for a winter wedding and, mixed with red and green blooms in this way, produces a warm and festive theme. (Some churches are strict about whom they allow to decorate and arrange flowers for ceremonies and many have a team of flower arrangers who like to be involved in the wedding decorations. Check with the priest or minister about the protocol in your chosen church.)

LEFT Jane and Ewan leaving the church after signing the register. Jane carries a simply tied bouquet of phalaenopsis orchids. **ABOVE** Ewan wears traditional Scottish dress – a Hunting Ogilvy tartan kilt with kilt pin, cream socks with green flashes and his Sgain Dubh (stocking knife).

For the reception, Jane and Ewan chose a site which happened to be decorated in a very rich red. Because Jane loves 'Grand Prix' roses, she developed a floral scheme around these, to complement the décor, including rich green celosia, green and red cymbidium orchids, and long red Singapore orchids. All the arrangements followed this luxurious festive theme, echoing the displays that were created for the church.

The table decorations were created in two heights, with half being high candelabras containing chunky square candles and half being low, square arrangements around huge square five-wick candles, giving a romantic feel to the reception. The tall arrangements were constructed by binding branches of *Hebe* to heavy metal candelabras so they looked like a living topiary. Floral foam was added to the top, and the striking 'Liberty' and 'Grand Prix' roses, along with amaryllis, celosia, Singapore orchids, and cymbidium orchids were added in groups. A ring of flowers was added to the base to conceal the heavy metal plate.

The lower arrangements were constructed using a square of foamboard which was cut to give a 2-inch (5-cm) edge of foam around the candle. Groups of 'Liberty' and 'Grand Prix' roses, amaryllis, celosia, Singapore orchids, and cymbidium orchids were added with *Hebe* and ivy berries completing the seasonal theme. In addition to the table arrangements, floral displays for the bar and other vases around the venue followed the same scheme.

LEFT These tall candelabras, covered in *Hebe* and topped with roses and orchids, don't prevent conversation across the table since the stem is thin. Candlelight is very flattering and adds to the ambiance of any party. **ABOVE RIGHT** The best man, guiding the guests and checking on his notes for the speech. Like Ewan, the groomsmen wore traditional Scottish dress. **BELOW LEFT** Jane and Ewan have a moment to reflect in the park under autumnal trees. The moth orchids in Jane's hair have been wired individually and positioned by Jane's hairdresser. **BELOW RIGHT** Flared-footed glass vases of red and green, including the trailing *Euphorbia fulgens*, are perfect for winter weddings.

"We couldn't have asked for anything more beautiful than the sight of our family and friends surrounded by the warm glow of candlelight and masses of incredible velvety roses." JANE

winter wedding

an intimate breakfast

shared with a small number of invited guests was the special choice of gourmets Shelly-Ann and Stuart for their wedding. They picked Raymond Blanc's restaurant, Le Manoir aux Quat' Saisons, near Oxford, as a site—not only for its fabulous food and renowned hospitality, but also for its accessibility.

Shelly-Ann's family are originally from Trinidad, and she wanted to reflect her ancestry in her wedding flowers, at the same time keeping the decorations very contemporary and smart. Shelly-Ann's personal preference for a simple, elegant look is reflected both in her stunning dress and the floral arrangements, and this consistent reflection of the bride's individuality is the key to a successful theme. Shelly-Ann loves white calla lilies and green orchids and *Anthurium*, so a cool white-and-green theme using lots of exotic fruits and foliage became the look of their very individual wedding. Howea palm, *Monstera*, and *Anthurium* leaves mixed with *Phormium*, papyrus, and trailing date palms added texture and shape to the arrangements. Star fruit and lime kumquats were used throughout the table arrangements, and pillar candles were covered with *Equisetum* to give the table a lush tropical effect. Large cube vases were lined with flax, while white calla lilies, cymbidium orchids, and date palm created a sumptuous feel, and reflected the choice of flowers of the bridal party. Both Stuart and Shelly-Ann liked the effect of using fruits in glass containers, and this seemed appropriate for their gourmet setting. Glass is extremely versatile, and can be used in many ways to suit classic or modern receptions. Le Manoir has lovely gardens and the private rooms where the ceremony and dinner were to be held were entered through two stone columns—the perfect place to arrange two garlands in the white-and-green theme with more tropical foliage.

Once inside the private rooms, Stuart and Shelly-Ann wanted to create a more sensuous ambiance, with candlelight and lots of tropical fruits and flowers in huge flared vases, such as red alpinia gingers from Trinidad, *Equisetum*, *Monstera* leaves, and brush papyrus. The romantic lighting and lush floral decoration brought a warmth to the ceremony, which was in perfect contrast to the crisp winter weather.

LEFT The bridegroom, looking very handsome in his purple suit, strides up to the ceremony accompanied by guests attired in traditional Scottish costume. **ABOVE** Shelly-Ann chose a simple dress. Because she is very tall, she chose a simply tied over-the-arm bouquet of white calla lilies, which most suited her style and gown and created an elegant look.

ABOVE LEFT Cymbidium orchids were given to each guest to wear for the day. **ABOVE CENTRE** *Alpinia* edged with papyrus and *Monstera* leaves in a vase lined with *Equisetum* make a sleek pedestal for the intimate ceremony. **ABOVE RIGHT** The groom's formal dress suits the exclusive site and Shelly-Ann's elegant look. **LEFT** The columns of the private dining area have ridges, which make them perfect for arranging collars of flowers. Howea palm leaves and *Phormium* are woven through the design, created on floral foam racks, to enhance the circular look. **BELOW** Trailing arrangements for the top table include striped fronds of date palm.

OPPOSITE The reception arrangements for the wedding breakfast were filled with lime kumquats and topped with 'Midori' anthuriums, white calla lilies, slipper and cymbidium orchids, and rich tropical foliage. LEFT Elegant slipcovers matching the tablecloth always make a room look very smart and bridal. Three cube vases were placed down the center of a long oblong table, and candles covered in *Equisetum* and masses of votives were dotted along the center of the dining table. BELOW LEFT *Phormium* and calla lilies mixed with a 'Midori' *Anthurium* and date palms, make a perfect chairback to suit the theme. BELOW RIGHT The bridal party pose for pictures.

"The floral arrangements were, without doubt, the highlight of our day. They created exactly the sensual ambiance we had hoped to achieve during the ceremony, which was really magical." STUART

Fresh flowers enhance your wedding in every way, but the one floral accessory everyone will remember is the bride's bouquet. Choosing the flowers for your bouquet will be one of the most pleasant pre-wedding tasks you will have to perform. You should be able to work with your florist to create a unique bouquet which is perfect for you and which you can comfortably carry to your ceremony. It will be the most photographed floral arrangement on the day and it should complement you and your chosen gown in every way.

Bridal bouquets began in medieval times as a small nosegay of sweetly scented flowers. Over the years they have changed and expanded and in Victorian times they became a wedding essential. The growth of the floristry business and the development of the skills of individual florists in the last century have made it possible that you can have a bouquet fashioned into just about any shape you like. Each flower head can be individually wired and the shape then constructed. The bouquet can take the form of a half moon, a curved pear, a heart, or even a letter of the alphabet. Wiring flowers also makes them lighter, and the handle of the bouquet will be thinner and neater in most cases. It can often be advantageous for the bride to request a wired bouquet. A heavy bouquet can become uncomfortable over the length of the wedding day.

By far the most common shape for a bouquet, however, is the tear-shaped cascade bouquet or shower. Although these are generally thought to be quite traditional, there are ways of making them contemporary, and in the hands of a skilled florist these bouquets can become very individual and imaginative. If you require a shower or cascade bouquet, it is possible to have the flowers bound with their natural stems, but sometimes it is best to have them wired together. There are two main reasons for this. Some flowers are simply too short and need to be wired to gain the extra length required. Others are too fragile and they will last better if they are wired and taped into place.

choosing the flowers
There are no hard-and-fast rules about wedding flowers, and it really is up to your own personal taste as to what you choose. In recent years there has been a trend for a simple round hand-tied bouquet on natural stems, usually of the same colored roses tied with a matching ribbon. (The wedding press has inadvertently contributed to making this style fashionable by commissioning a number of these bouquets from florists.) The advantage is that they are relatively easy and quick to create and always photograph well, however they are held!

The natural, just-picked collection of flowers has also been popular, as well as the inclusion of herbs in a bouquet using favorites such as lavender, rosemary, sage, lemon balm, myrtle, and scented eucalyptus.

Choosing which flowers to have in your bridal bouquet is extremely personal. Some brides have flowers that are symbolic of their relationship with their husband-to-be. Brides wearing antique dresses or family heirlooms very often wish to style a bouquet from their family album and may bring in a portrait from which to take inspiration. To get an insight into the bouquet that you think you might be comfortable holding, it is a good idea to browse through wedding magazines and books and look for ideas that appeal. After some time, you should start to build up an idea of the design you like, and it will be easier to discuss this with your florist if you make use of clippings—particularly as most people's botanical knowledge is limited!

color Of course the overwhelming majority of brides now choose to get married in white but this was not always the case. This particular custom became popular only in the Victorian period. If your dress is white or ivory, whether you choose white or a color for your flowers may depend on what kind of look you are trying to create. If you are planning a really formal wedding you will probably choose an all-white bouquet of one type of flower or a combination. You may decide to pick one of the more traditional flowers: lily-of-the-valley, gardenias, stephanotis, peonies, freesias, calla lilies, tulips, orchids, or—of course—roses.

If you do decide to choose white, there is an enormous range of shades within this one color. The whitest blooms are moth orchids. Sweet peas and 'Akito' roses, gardenias, and calla lilies can be quite creamy. White does always look sophisticated and is the most traditional choice. It is also symbolic of purity, and the lily, in particular, symbolizes innocence. Brides marrying for the second time may therefore shy away from this choice of flower. Some brides worry that white flowers on white fabric will be lost, but most bouquets are edged with foliage

OPPOSITE An informal round bouquet of fragrant summer flowers including *Alchemilla mollis* and *Gypsophila* with 'Blue Moon' and 'Deep Secret' garden roses and sweet peas.
ABOVE (CLOCKWISE FROM TOP LEFT) A classic, delicate bouquet of white 'Akito' roses combined with scented lily-of-the-valley and edged with lily-of-the-valley leaves; This alternative bouquet of white calla lilies encircled with white ostrich feathers makes a striking contemporary arrangement, which fulfils the bride's fairytale theme and complements her dress; A flamboyant shower bouquet using groups of textural flowers including velvety 'Grand Prix' red roses, poppy seed heads, and the balls of *Viburnum opulus*, mixed with the exotic heads of cymbidium orchids and spikes of 'James Storei' Singapore orchids edged with fronds of fern.

which lifts them from the dress material. Unsurprisingly, most dress designers, if asked, would recommend white flowers, as this often shows off their dresses to the best advantage! They often advise using delicate bouquets for the same reason.

Some brides feel uncomfortable at the thought of wearing all white and carrying white flowers, and prefer to pick a pale or pastel color. They can also pick this up in their make up and nail polish. It is true that if you have a very colorful bouquet, the eye will be drawn to the flowers. So if you are a "shrinking violet" and nervous of being the center of attention choose a vibrant collection of flowers for your bouquet.

If you have chosen to wear any color other than white, this will obviously affect your choice of flowers too. (From a very young age I always saw myself in a pink gown. As the old rhyme says, "Married in pink, of you he will always think!") But in the end I opted for traditional ivory, using the flowers to express my love of pink. ("Married in white, she has chosen right!") If you choose to go down the aisle in a rich or dark colored fabric, a brightly colored bunch will be better suited. Some predominantly white bridal gowns include colored embroidery or faux flowers which may also lead to the use of color.

BELOW (LEFT TO RIGHT) The tradition of passing on the good fortune of the bride by throwing the bridal bouquet is still very popular and is a perfect end to the wedding festivities. It is the custom for whoever catches the bouquet to keep it, but some brides choose to preserve their bouquets. This may not always be possible and depends very much on the choice of flowers and their condition at the end of the day.

When considering which colors you can put together you can choose a range of pastel shades, monochromatic schemes (in which flowers of different types but the same color are used together), a two-tone color theme, or a really vibrant scheme with a bright combination of rich and dark colors mixed together. Your florist will be able to show you examples of different combinations in varied forms and will be your best counsel on what will work best for you.

In the main, less formal and casual weddings are more likely to use color and to include a larger assortment of flower types. The time of year will influence your choice of color, as will the time of day your wedding is planned. A lunchtime wedding in spring suggests white or a pastel color. A midsummer celebration, going on into the evening, may take advantage of the deep pinks, blues, and lilacs of the time of year. A winter wedding on a cold and dark day may be brought to life with the warmth of ruby red or jewel-coloured anemones. Personally, although I think white can be the most sophisticated choice, I tend to feel happier with a color, so I think it is imperative that the bride makes the decision of white versus color for herself!

Once you've chosen your bouquet, ask your florist to deliver the flowers to coincide with the arrival of the photographer at your home. (Do not request an earlier delivery, as you need to keep your flowers as fresh as possible and it is best to leave them with the professionals for as long as you can.) When they arrive, they will be nestled into tissue in a box and it is best to place them in the coolest part of your house until you are dressed and ready for your photographs.

making your own

If you decide that you would like to create your own flower arrangements for your wedding, it is probably best to stick to a simple theme using one type of flower only—roses, calla lilies, sweet peas or hydrangea are good choices. Another consideration is that some flowers may be simple to use but can be tricky to keep in good condition —moth orchids (*Phalaenopsis*), for example—so it is advisable to leave more fussy specimens to the professional florist.

Make sure that you condition your flowers well so that they are in peak condition on your special day. (Give them a good long soak in tepid water mixed with flower food, the day before your ceremony.) Arrange them simply, looking in the mirror to help you get the desired shape and to make sure that they are an appropriate size for you to hold. Then trim with a lovely sash or bow. Keep them in water until about twenty minutes before you are ready to go, then dry them off carefully.

If you want to cover the handle with ribbon then the best way is to tape the stems together with white floral tape, and then add two strips of double-coated sticky tape down the length of the stems, round the bottom, and up the other side. This will make it easier for you to place one piece of ribbon down the handle and across the ends of the stems. You can then cover the handle in circles of ribbon, starting from the top down to the base and then returning to the top. Place a pearl-headed pin in the end of the ribbon just beneath the flower heads, and then trim the end of the ribbon carefully. Finally, trim the bound stem with a bow under the flower heads to conceal the pin.

If you are making your own bouquet and want to pick mainly seasonal flowers, then for spring I recommend narcissi, jasmine, lily-of-the-valley, camelliats, hyacinths, or freesias. Other possibilities are violets, grape hyacinths, ranunculus, and seasonal blossoms such as guelder roses and lilacs. In summer my favorites for bouquets are garden roses, sweet peas, stephanotis florets, peonies, lilies, and, gardenia blooms. In late summer, I love to use calla lilies, nerines, hydrangeas, and vibrant flowers such as morning glories, gerberas, and dahlias mixed with rose hips and early berries such as snowberries and *Hypericum*. In winter, you can use trailing foliage to great advantage—I love to mix it with roses, seed heads, and berries. For a simpler look, use orchids (but remember, these may be difficult to keep in good condition); or for a really delicate feel, the tiny flower heads of hellebores are perfect for Christmas brides.

catching and conserving the bouquet The custom of
throwing your bouquet at the end of the festivities dates back to the eighteenth century, when it was thought to pass on the good fortune of the bride and groom to anyone who was lucky enough to catch the flowers. This was quite a serious tradition in the days when a woman was considered the property of, first, her father and then her husband after marriage. For these women, marriage was necessary to secure their own financial security. We have moved on a long way from those days, but the custom of throwing the bouquet remains a lovely highlight of the end of the festivities. (If you can't bear to part with your bridal bouquet, an alternate idea is to have a second "throwing bouquet" created specially for this part of the celebration. It is even possible to have the throwing bouquet made up as an part of your main arrangement, to be detached when the appropriate time comes.)

Finally, if you catch the bouquet you may wish to try to conserve it for the bride. Some brides wish to make the bouquet a lasting memento of their day and may ask for advice on which flowers preserve best. Personally, I think that long-term preservation is not a good basis on which to select your wedding flowers! In truth, I think the best way of doing this is to use a professional company who preserve or press bridal bouquets. (I preserved some from my own wedding, and it is a lovely keepsake.) However be warned that, over time, all plant material exposed to the light will start to degrade and lose its true color. Whatever kind of preservation method you select, it only looks really good for the first few years, so don't let this desire to preserve your petals for posterity rule your overall choices! Just have what you like best and make the most of your special day!

ABOVE (CLOCKWISE FROM TOP LEFT)
This petite variety of calla lily (*Zantedeschia aethiopica*) has been specially developed for weddings. The classic shower shape suits a princess-style gown; The choice of a rich color for your bridal gown will be perfectly complemented by a vibrant mix of rich flowers; A concentric-circle bouquet using sweet peas edged with *Viburnum opulus* and trimmed with curled aspidistra leaves.

the shape of your bouquet

Generally speaking, the shape of your bouquet will be determined largely by your dress style and shape. There are basically three styles of bouquet you can choose from: the round bouquet, the long, trailing shower bouquet, and the over-arm bouquet.

An elaborate dress with a wide skirt and cathedral-length veil suits a flamboyant and large bouquet. Masses of silk taffeta and tulle need a long bouquet of a traditional nature. This is more likely to be wired to get the length and may use many varieties of flowers. A slender cut of dress will suit a more structured, longer and thinner bouquet. Calla lilies, moth orchids, or even *Anthurium* are suitable for this style of gown. An empire-line or Victorian-style dress will suit a round bouquet of one type of flowers or groups of flowers arranged tightly together. Alternatively, choose a Victorian or Biedermeier, made from concentric circles of flowers in coordinating colors.

You must also consider your own size. If you are, tall you may need a longer-stemmed look for an over-arm bouquet or extra length if you choose a trailing bouquet.

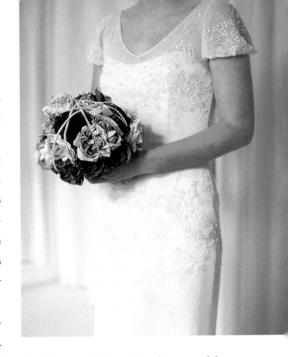

If you are petite, you may end up looking overwhelmed by a huge armful of flowers, and a long shower bouquet might not suit your style of dress.

To assist my brides in choosing their bouquet, I often accompany them to one of their earlier dress fittings and take some flowers so we can start to decide what suits the dress best. This also gives the bride a chance to see how different flowers look with the backdrop of the skirt of her gown. It helps to involve your florist in the wedding plans, to give her a chance to see the look you want and to gain insight into your personality and style. Your florist will give you advice based on a number of factors: your stature, coloring, and personality, as well as your gown. She will steer you from impractical ideas and guide you towards flowers that last well.

LEFT This grand, white shower bouquet would suit an extravagant wedding and perfectly suit a full skirt and long train. The gardenia and stephanotis flowers have been wired into this trailing design. Because of the length of time required to create this style of bouquet and the number of perfect flower heads that have been used, it is an expensive option to choose. This bouquet not only looks stunning but also has a fabulous scent from both the stephanotis and gardenia, which are often chosen as the key scents for perfume. **ABOVE** The recent trend for dinner party weddings has contributed to a fashion for more glitzy bridal gowns, often decorated with beads, jewels, and crystals. This beautiful dress has been complemented with rich pink garden roses encircled by *faux* diamonds, which pick up the jeweled theme of the gown. A round bouquet is perfectly suited to this straight skirt.

CLOCKWISE FROM RIGHT Full skirts and long trains suit longer and larger bouquets. Here open 'Shirley Temple' peonies have been hand-tied into a teardrop shape. Massed flowers of one type have recently been the most popular choice for weddings and are perhaps one of the most successful options because they photograph well; Lace or heavy brocade fabric is often complemented by the use of rich colors or heavily textural flowers. The lace fabric of this beautiful gown contains a rose motif, complemented perfectly by the open petals of a bouquet of mixed garden roses, which suit the very decorative nature of the gown; Here, innocent-looking daisies (*Gerbera* 'Pinky Eye') perfectly complement the disarming simplicity of this dress.

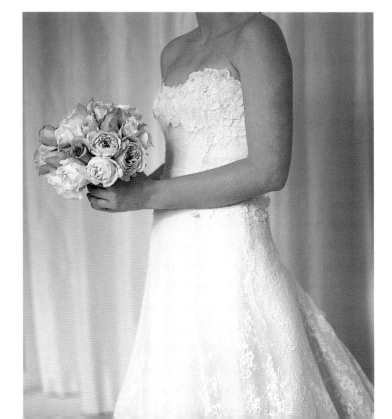

the perfect choice

A fabulous bridal bouquet can be created with almost any flower; your options are limited only by your imagination, the seasonal availability of flowers, and the skills of your florist. A truly professional florist works at a number of budget ranges and will be sympathetic to your own personal style, working with you to create the most appropriate bouquet for your special day. Often there is one flower that may run through the theme of the wedding and appear in the bride's bouquet, the attendants' bouquets, the boutonnieres, and even the centerpieces for the reception. If this works, out that is fine, but I always advise my brides to go with what suits their dress the best and worry less about coordinating all the other floral decorations with the bridal bouquet.

Any color can be incorporated into a bouquet; often the final choice is based on the bridesmaids' gowns, a color that is most complementary to the bride, or simply a favorite flower or color. Other factors that might influence your decision are the time of year when your wedding is taking place and the look you choose for the ceremony—formal or informal, traditional, or contemporary.

Once you've decided on the perfect shape and color scheme for your bouquet, make sure that it coordinates perfectly with your gown by using the same fabric to wrap the stem, or, alternatively, give a swatch to your florist so they can trim your bouquet with a ribbon to match your dress. Your florist will also be able to advise you on how to hold your bouquet to show it at its best. Check this in a full-length mirror before you leave home, so that you point the flowers towards the photographer and make the most of them in your photographs. A good professional photographer will help you to look your best.

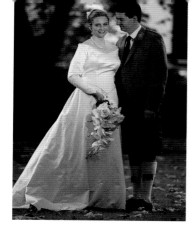

OPPOSITE LEFT A round, natural bouquet of mixed colors like this is very popular for summer brides. Lilac, blue, and cream roses have been mixed with *Viburnum opulus*. OPPOSITE RIGHT This is a large, round bouquet of open peony blooms, which is very suited to the choice of a formal city site. THIS PAGE (CLOCKWISE FROM ABOVE) Moth orchids are a very popular choice for brides who would like to have a trailing bouquet but don't want to have anything too formal or fussy. These long stems of orchids can be simply tied together, and they come in a variety of colors from magenta pink to cinnamon gold; Compact bouquets of one type of flower are very easy to hold and are by far the most popular choice of bridal bouquet. Here the chocolate cosmos pick up the detail of the dress; Keeping the stems longer requires the bride to hold the bouquet either upright (bottom right) or over the arm (below), as shown with these two different bouquets featuring calla lilies.

the flowers

The choice of flowers for your bridal bouquet is often one of the hardest decisions to make because it will be your most important accessory, and it is essential that it complement both your dress and your personality. You may choose to use flowers that are symbolic of your relationship or simply your favorite varieties. I think a scented bouquet is lovely; I like to use lily-of-the-valley, stephanotis, garden roses, or gardenias.

OPPOSITE Fluffy white peonies 'Duchesse de Nemours' hand tied into a simple bouquet and edged with hosta leaves. **THIS PAGE** A mixed summer bouquet includes 'Sarah Bernhardt' peonies, pale pink *Astilbe* 'Erica', mock orange *Philadelphus* 'Virginal', double white lisianthus (*Eustoma grandiflorum* 'Echo Pure White') and 'Aretha' (a bi-color Ecuadorian rose).

THIS PAGE This classic wired bouquet is made entirely of stephanotis, which is beautifully fragrant and always popular. The star-shaped flowers are individually wired and arranged with camellia leaves around the edge. The wires creating the handle are covered in satin ribbon. OPPOSITE A rich and brightly colored bouquet created for a bride who chose deep purple for her wedding gown. The design is spiraled and tied. It includes the fashionable burgundy rose 'Black Baccara', the pink rose 'Milano', and *Viburnum opulus*. Purple lisianthus adds movement with its lovely tendrils and buds. The pink and yellow *Gloriosa* pull together the pink and acid green. It is edged with glossy green camellia leaves and finished with a purple satin bow.

THIS PAGE An autumnal grouped bouquet including huge ornamental cabbage (*Brassica oleracea* 'Sunrise '99'), balanced against groups of three velvety 'Grand Prix' roses, hydrangea flower heads (*Hydrangea macrophylla* 'Rotshwartz'), rose hips (*Rosa* 'Sensation'), and seeded eucalyptus. **OPPOSITE** An over-arm bouquet of white calla lilies and green *Anthurium* 'Midori' edged with dark *Ligularia* leaves is tied with white ribbon.

Small, delicate flowers as shown on these two pages, require a generous number of stems to look effective. **OPPOSITE** A massed bouquet of lily-of-the-valley, such as this featuring the pure white species *Convallaria majalis*, requires hundreds of spires of the sweet-scented flower to create an impact. Although lily-of-the-valley is available all the year round, grown under glass, it is generally at its best, most plentiful and less expensive in springtime. **THIS PAGE** Delicate velvety, chocolate cosmos (*Cosmos atrosanguineus* 'Black Beauty') are prized for their deep color and their heavenly scent of chocolate—the perfect choice for a chocoholic!

how to make a rose dome bouquet

The round bouquet is a classic shape which works well with most styles of wedding gown, and it is also often held by flowergirls or bridesmaids. This shape also photographs very well, which is perhaps why it is so popular with the bridal media. It is less time-consuming and costly to put together than a wired shower bouquet, and so florists often prefer to prepare these designs when they are invited to send bouquets in for fashion shoots, rather than more complicated and intricate designs.

Rose domes are created by hand-tying a selection of roses. If you wish to use one color you can make a massed design or you can mix colors. Add greenery and foliage to the dome itself or around the edge of the bouquet. For simple rose domes of one color I usually edge them with camellia or galax leaves, or folded aspidistra leaves. If I am mixing fillers and foliage, with roses my favorite greens are the vibrant hues of *Viburnum opulus*, which is most plentiful in spring when it is naturally in season but which can be bought (at a cost) at other times of the year, or *Alchemilla mollis*, which is available in the summer when *Viburnum opulus* becomes more difficult to get. I am also very fond of the star-shaped *Astrantia* to complement roses, and love the pink or silver version.

You can finish a bouquet by either leaving the stems natural and trimming them with a bow around the binding point, or by covering the handle with ribbon secured with double-coated tape.

MATERIALS

40 garden roses (mixed colors)
5 stems of *Viburnum opulus*
Reel of double-coated tape
Green gutta-percha tape
String
Ribbon
Scissors
Knife

HOW TO

1 First clean your roses and remove all the lower foliage. Strip the rose stems of thorns. Take a sharp knife and gently prise them off by moving the blade down the length of the stem.

2 Take a central rose and—holding it between your thumb and first finger—add flowers at an angle to the left-hand side. Add about five flowers and then twist the bunch (using your right hand to move it but keeping it in your left hand). Add a further five flowers and twist again.

3 Tie your bouquet tightly underneath the flower heads, so that it is firmly held together, and then trim all the stems to the width of your hand. Tie again at the bottom of the stems to form the handle and then, starting from the base of the heads, bind to the tip with gutta-percha tape.

4 To hide the stems, run double-coated tape down either side, and cover lengthwise with two to four strips of ribbon. Add another strip around the handle, working from the top to the bottom and then back to the top. Secure with a bow made from three loops and one central ribbon.

how to make a victorian nosegay

Much of Victorian design is both neat and fussy in its detail, and this floral arrangement of concentric circles of flowers is known as a Victorian nosegay in the flower world. The use of a number of different flowers in a rigid design was often highly symbolic, and designed to convey a specific meaning. (Very little of this "floral language" is used today in our choice of flowers and plants, but much of the symbolism remains.) It was during this time that the floristry profession started to emerge. Very often these "florists" were gardeners attached to large estates and gardens, who learnt to wire individual heads from flowers to create more complicated and intricate designs. Wiring flowers allows you to have much more control over them, and so the idea of creating a wired concentric-circle nosegay became very fashionable. In keeping with much of nineteenth-century design, these nosegays were quite fussy, and would include a number of smaller flowers wired and then placed in circles around a larger central flower. Wiring is very time consuming, and you have to work very close to the deadline of the event, because the flowers are removed from the stem and are no longer able to take up water.

Here, I have shown how to make a Victorian nosegay without any wire, and the key to success is choosing the right flowers to create this design. Small-headed flowers such as violets, forget-me-nots, grape hyacinth, narcissus, pinks, sweet peas, and roses are very suitable.

MATERIALS

10 bunches of grape hyacinths (*Muscari*)
3 bunches of sweet peas
12 'Vendela' roses
2 bunches of forget-me-nots
1 central rose
Scissors
Strong tape
Ribbon

HOW TO

1 First, clean all the foliage and thorns from the roses, and clean the forget-me nots. Carefully arrange the forget-me-nots around the central rose in your left hand. Keep turning the bunch with your right hand as you are doing this, to enable you to make a neat circle of the blue flowers around the central single rose.

2 Next add the 'Vendela' roses just a little lower than the height of the forget-me-nots—creating the lovely domed shape. Make sure you place the roses at exactly the same height all around, to create a defined circular shape.

3 Next, you are ready to add the delicate sweet peas. Keep your left hand very relaxed as you add them and then use your right hand to move the bunch so that you are working on all sides.

4 Finally, add bunches of five grape hyacinths at a time, placing them lower than the sweet peas —continue working on all sides of the bunch. Work round three times in all (adding three layers of the grape hyacinths), so that you have a sumptuously bunched finshed effect.

creating a theme

In addition to her own bouquet, a bride may plan many other floral accessories, both for herself and for certain key members of the wedding party. The outfits for the groomsmen, ushers, bridesmaids, flower girls, ring-bearers, pages, and, of course, the immediate family all go toward creating the total look for her wedding day. Their clothes need to harmonize with the bride's dress and complement the overall theme of the wedding, and this is equally true of any floral accessories they wear. They should enhance but not outshine the bride!

flowers in the hair

Flowers worn by the bride in her hair on her wedding day can be one of the most exquisite accessories. Wearing a ring of flowers is a tradition that dates from Ancient Greece. Queen Victoria helped to revive this classic trend when she was married, wearing a crown of orange blossom; and in more recent times that epitome of style, the Hollywood actress Audrey Hepburn, wore a simple ring of rosebuds on her head for her wedding in 1954. This is the most popular floral accessory, and it should be planned in conjunction with your bouquet and will involve a collaboration between your hairdresser and your florist. Your choice of headdress will also be influenced by how you decide to wear your hair and whether or not you are going to wear a veil.

Brides can choose to wear a single large flower, a number of small wired florets (individual rosebuds or stephanotis, for example), a full headband, a floral circlet or a tiara, which is usually made from very delicate florets (such as hyacinths, stephanotis, or tuberose). A headband or a comb of flowers is most often worn in front of the veil and this is a clever technique for adding a little more to your height if you need to. In recent years jewelled tiaras have become more popular with brides for creating this effect, but many people still opt for a fresh floral headdress to complement their bouquet.

Fresh flowers near your face can make you look younger, your skin rosier, and your eyes brighter. It is, after all, probably the only time you are going to be able to wear flowers in your hair, and there is something wonderfully indulgent about bedecking yourself with fresh flowers. However, if you are planning a headdress it is important that you have a run through with your hairdresser and it is certainly worthwhile asking your florist to make a trial headdress for you, as you do not want any snags or surprises on the day!

Some brides may choose to wear a hat, and this can also be decorated with fresh flowers and foliage. Ideally, flowers should be placed on a wider brimmed hat. Midsummer brides or more informal brides may choose this option, and it is also often a popular choice for the more mature or second-time bride. Your florist will wire up the flowers and attach them to your hat and deliver the two together on your wedding day. Sometimes the mother of the bride or groom may choose this accessory instead of wearing a corsage. Matrons-of-honor may also prefer this, and some of your guests will like the idea, too.

necklaces and bracelets

It is customary in India to wear floral garlands around the neck or wrist and we often make these for weddings involving a mix of cultures. At a Hindu wedding, the bride and groom exchange sumptuous garlands, mainly of red and white flowers decorated with silver, assembled by threading the flower head onto wire. Carnations work well for these, as they are relatively inexpensive (a factor when so many flower heads are needed) and are durable.

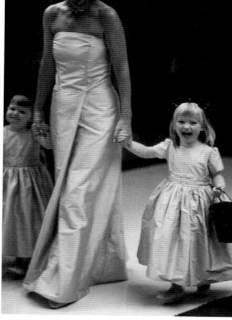

Some brides like to break with convention and wear something more unusual, such as a floral boa or a necklace of flowers. If you do choose a necklace, you need to have a good, elegant neck so experiment first! Wrist corsages can also add glamour to a bridal dress and look fabulous on more mature bridesmaids or matrons-of-honor. Some brides choose to have their shoes adorned with flowers which peep out from under the gown as they walk. If you are planning something out of the ordinary, it is worth spending a little bit more money and asking your florist to make you a prototype to try out. That way you can be sure you are happy with your ideas. If you wish to sew flower heads onto your dress, you will have to ask your florist to wire them, so that the stem is removed, making it easier for you to attach them to your gown. A few miniature rose heads sewn on to the veil can look very romantic.

Flowers aren't just for the bride! For one midsummer wedding in Italy I made a wild floral headdress for the groom as well as the bride. For another groom I made a floral adornment to wear as a scarf and even—for another incurable romantic —a Cupid's bow and arrow! The scope and nature of the floral accessories you can have at your wedding is limited only by your imagination and personal preference and the skill and creativity of the designer you are working with.

accessories for the young

Younger bridesmaids, flower girls, page boys, and young ring-bearers are often dressed more seasonally than the bride, with more attention to the time of year. In winter, bridesmaids may wear fake fur muffs decorated with flowers and page boys may be dressed in rich tartan or velvet. How you decide to dress your attendants will depend largely on their ages, the time of the year, and any theme you are planning for your wedding. Your contemporaries are not going to speak to you again if you dress them in a sugar-almond pink tutu and give them a set of iridescent wings and a floral wand, but your three-year-old niece will undoubtedly think it the highlight of the year! Floral headdresses are best for the youngest bridesmaids, and there are two types that are suitable for young children with especially fine hair—a circlet that goes all around the head and sits on the crown or a headband, where the flowers are wired onto a frame. It is a good idea to give your florist a size for the circlet as a guide. This measurement will

OPPOSITE Individually wiring flower heads and having your hairdresser pin them into your hair is a pretty way of using flowers as an accessory for adult bridesmaids or matrons-of-honor. The scented, star-shaped florets of stephanotis are perfect for this because they are quite waxy and long-lasting. **ABOVE, LEFT TO RIGHT** Classic willow bridesmaid's basket filled with white rosebuds, sweet peas, and stephanotis; Little sequinned bags filled with roses make an alternative to a basket. Again these type of floral accessories are perfect for a younger bridesmaid to carry as they can be put down.

depend on how the bridesmaid is going to wear it; however they are usually fastened with a hook, which can be adjusted on the day.

Sometimes a headband can be the most practical option since you can ask your bridesmaid to break one in before having your florist attach the flowers and deliver it on the day. You may even ask your dressmaker to cover a band with fabric to match the bridesmaids' dresses. Some bridesmaids are more stoical than others about wearing headdresses, and it is worth spending a little time thinking about this to avoid having a floral headdress cause a high drama just before your big moment. If you are lucky enough to have your hairdresser with you while you are dressing ask them to fit the floral headdresses for your attendants.

There is no limit to the floral accessories you can add to your wedding for your young attendants. For a festive wedding in winter I have created miniature Christmas trees and kissing balls fashioned from woven mistletoe for the bridesmaids to carry. At one late afternoon wedding in the fall the older pages carried storm lanterns, and for another, eight bridesmaids carried candles on brass trays decorated with ivies, which seemed quite adventurous but passed without incident! We have made hoops of rose hips and berries in the fall and baskeys of wheat and harvested fruits for a wedding in late September.

I have seen young bridesmaids dressed as fairies or miniature pre-Raphaelite beauties. To make your bridesmaids look like little Greek goddesses, use long *Ruscus* leaves and stephanotis florets to make a simple green-and-white headdress. One of my favorite accessories for a young bridesmaid is the flower ball or pomander. These can be created from moss or floral foam and look very cute. They also work well if the bride has chosen a dome of roses, as they match it. Ask your florist to wire and sew some flowers on your bridesmaids' shoes; this works particularly well with ballet shoes or satin slippers.

Page boys do not usually carry anything, although they often sport a miniature rosebud. Their costumes vary from the traditional and formal to military-inspired, with sailor suits still being a classic. Pages may be asked to carry a prayer book or a basket of petals to throw after the ceremony. Flowers are wired and attached to the book as a marker. Traditionally these accessories were made from white flowers, either a mixture of roses and orchids or a single type of flower, such as the beautiful, and appropriately named, Easter lily. Ring bearers often have a cushion made from moss or flower heads to take to the altar.

THIS PAGE A hand-held hurricane lamp is decorated with ivy and three open 'Queensday' roses. Other unusual accessories include floral wands for 'fairies', teddy bears, moss cushions for ring bearers, sprays for prayer books, leis, and flower boas, a shepherdess's crook and a Cupid's bow and arrow for a ring bearer.

baskets of flowers

Baskets filled with cut flowers are a very popular bridesmaid's accessory. One of the main advantages of a basket is that it allows the bridesmaid to put down her flowers when necessary, whereas a bouquet if constantly handled can become damaged around the edges and start to droop. Baskets of petals are also very popular, and attendants can sprinkle petals on the floor before the entrance of the bride to create a gorgeous scent. Alternatively, rose petals can be put into pretty paper cones and handed out to all the guests to scatter at the end of the ceremony.

choosing flowers for your attendants

When choosing flowers for your attendants to carry, remember that they should complement your overall scheme and be appropriate to your attendants' outfits and size, as you do not want to overburden them. An experienced florist will advise you on this. Most often bridesmaids carry smaller bouquets, as this is the least expensive option. The flowers are usually more colorful than the bridal bouquet and are made in proportion to the size of the person carrying them, so be sure to let your designer know their ages. Make sure that your chief bridesmaid shows the smaller attendants how to hold their flowers, and to keep their arms relaxed so that they look their best as they walk into the ceremony.

boutonnieres
As well as other wedding flowers it is customary to order special boutonnieres for your fiancé, his father, and grandfather and your father, the best man, and all the ushers. These boutonnieres usually chosen to suit the men's ties and the other flowers, so white is often the safest and easiest option, though you might pick a special color for your own father and fiancé. Although it is a lovely idea to want to give all your guests a floral accessory such as a boutonniere it is quite expensive and can be needlessly extravagant. In my experience, very often people do not want to pin a flower onto their outfit, so these gifts are passed by. If you are going to make this gesture, make sure you appoint a particular usher to offer the boutonnieres to each guest as they arrive at the ceremony, and make sure your florist has labelled any special flowers so that they can be offered to the appropriate person.

decorating bags
It is traditional for mothers and grandmothers of the happy couple to have larger boutonnieres or corsages to wear. These are usually chosen to suit their outfits and may be pinned onto handbags to protect their clothes. If you want a florist to do this, it is essential to check that the bag is suitable; it works best if the bag is rigid, rather than a soft fabric. Leave it with the designer and ask them to have it delivered decorated on the day. For a handbag corsage, I love to use gardenias or roses, which can be wired onto the strap or across the front if it is clutch style. Single orchids or smaller sprays of blooms (often known collectively as Singapore orchids) are perfect for corsages, as they are very durable and long lasting and come in a huge range of colors. For a sweetly scented corsage, you can choose freesias, stephanotis, garden roses, or gardenia. If a bag corsage isn't appropriate, a flower to trim a hat is a good alternative to wearing a corsage or boutonniere. A flower wired into the hair is another possibility, and for sleeveless dresses a wrist corsage is also an option to consider.

You can adorn all parents, grandparents, siblings, and special guests with flowers as a symbol of unity with your new family and as a way of letting all the rest of the guests know who is special!

ABOVE (CLOCKWISE FROM TOP LEFT) It used to be traditional for the host to provide boutonnieres for all the guests but now it is more common for boutonnieres and corsages to be bought for the immediate family and the ushers only. Orchid corsages, such as this one, are very popular for mothers and grandmothers; The most popular choice for boutonnieres for male attendants is a simple rose with foliage, and white 'Avalanche' is the safest color to pick for your ushers; Often the bridegroom's boutonniere will coordinate with a flower from the bridal bouquet. This is a classic rose boutonniere ('Bianca Candy') with seasonal foliage of snowberries (*Symphoricarpos* x *doorenbosii* 'Red Pearl').

pretty in pink

an impressive venue can really set the tone of a wedding. When Jenny and Tim decided to marry, they were one of a select few couples who are lucky enough to enjoy the honor of holding their ceremony in the crypt of St. Paul's Cathedral, London, as Tim's father has been awarded a CBE. On one of her earliest visits to my shop, Jenny picked out a deep pink calla lily for her own bouquet, which inspired the overall cream and pink floral theme. This was carried through to the other wedding flowers, which included the creamy 'Vendela' rose and 'Laminuette', which is a cream rose edged with pink. Jenny then spent a long time tracking down the fabric for her bridesmaids' dresses to match her bridal flowers. She finally found soft, dusky-pink shot silk. For herself, she decided to have a simple hand-tied shower of the long-stemmed calla lilies she had originally chosen to carry on the day. To coordinate with Jenny, Tim wore a 'Black Baccara' rose boutonniere, while each of the groomsmen wore 'Vendela' roses.

For the chapel, we decorated round privet trees with roses and then positioned two large pedestals and decorations at the ends of the pews. Following the ceremony, the bridal party were taken to a naval and military club for a cocktail party with 200 guests, canapés, the speeches, and the champagne toast, as well as the cutting of the cake. They then settled down for the wedding breakfast with a more intimate group of family, since the venue had limited space for dinner. For this richly colored room, Jenny chose to have lots of candlelight, so to make an impression on half the tables we used tall copper candelabras, each holding eight candles. On the other half of the tables we had low arrangements of glass cubes that were themselves surrounded by individual candlelights and then filled with *Equisetum* topped with sweet peas, roses, and lisianthus.

ABOVE Jenny and Tim steal a kiss after the ceremony. Tim's tie and boutonniere match Jenny's beautiful shower bouquet of pink calla lilies perfectly, while his green vest harmonzies with the rich green foliage used throughout for the floral accessories.

The flowers had to be removed from St. Paul's immediately after the ceremony, so we were able to re-use them at the reception site. While the guests were enjoying their drinks and canapés we brought the flowers in through the back door and garlanded the stairs with the flowers which had been used to decorate the pew ends at the church. Many more of Jenny and Tim's friends returned after the family dinner, and even more joined them to dance the night away in a marquee that had been erected in an adjoining courtyard.

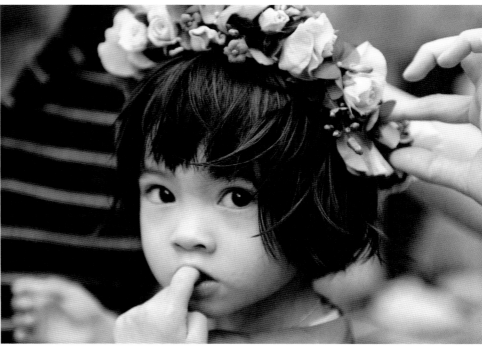

CLOCKWISE FROM ABOVE The bridal party leave the ceremony, Jenny holding her shower bouquet of calla lilies and the bridesmaids wearing circlets of roses and sweet peas; An apprehensive bridesmaid tries out her floral headdress. It's a good idea to ask your bridesmaid to break in a headdress before decorating it for the ceremony; Jenny and Tim smiling at their guests as they leave the chapel. Jenny's beautiful shower bouquet suits a formal setting such as this, and looks perfect with her classic gown and long veil; Tim's groomsmen line up on the steps of the church, sporting their 'Vendela' rose boutonnieres. Tailored jackets such as these often have a small loop behind the lapel to anchor the boutonniere.

"Paula's flowers were an inspiration and she made sure that every detail was perfect on the day." JENNY

CLOCKWISE FROM LEFT The bridal party snatch time for a photograph in a nearby garden square. You can see the youngest bridesmaid has already dispensed with her floral headdress! The Matron of Honor carried a nosegay of sweet peas, which are a personal favorite of mine for their delicacy, their enormous diversity of color, and above all their divine scent; Professional boutonnieres and corsages have a pearl-headed pin attached to them to secure them onto the lapel. The pin should be used at the back so that it is out of sight but keeps the flower firmly in place; A three-tiered cake with pillars is decorated with flowers and (as befits a military and naval club) a sword is on hand for the first cut, when the bride and groom make their wishes for their life together. The cake was decorated with three arrangements of sweet peas, roses, and lisianthus with a dark green *Ruscus* garland around the table. For small arrangements like these, I often use the bottom of a foam cup to hold a piece of floral foam in which the flowers can be arranged; Family and friends take their seats for the wedding breakfast under candelabras filled with roses, lisianthus, sweet peas, and calla lilies.

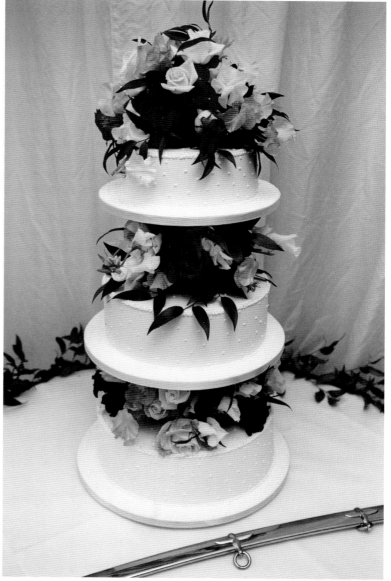

boutonnieres

thistle with berries

A late summer boutonniere of black-eyed Susan seedheads (*Rudbeckia hirta*) with montbretia berries (*Crocosmia* 'Lucifer') and backed with three smoke bush leaves (*Cotinus coggygria* 'Royal Purple').

red & pink

A simple rose boutonniere (*Rosa* 'Jacaranda') can be made more seasonal and exotic by adding a celosia head (*Celosia* var. *cristata* 'No. 9') brown alder berries (*Alnus*), and black *Viburnum tinus* berries.

spiky bloom

Round-shaped flowers, such as this medium-sized single dahlia (*Dahlia* 'Bishop of Llandaff'), make perfect boutonnieres. Other good round shapes include smaller gerberas known as 'Germini', miniature sunflowers (*Helianthus annuus*), ranunculus, and daisies such as *Leucanthemum vulgare*.

calla & berries

This ever-popular mix of deep pink calla lilies (*Zantedeschia aethiopica* 'Majestic Red') and *Hypericum* berries is often chosen to match the bridal bouquet. Calla lilies have a beautiful flower shape and come in a wide range of colors, from deep burgundy, pink, lilac, yellow, and mango to white.

chilies

In fall there are a number of seedheads, berries, and ornamental vegetables that can be wired to make a boutonniere or corsage. Here, two sprigs of rose hips (*Rosa* 'Sensation') have been wired with two sprigs of vibrant *Capsicum annuum* and edged with wired dark leaves from the smoke bush plant (*Cotinus coggygria* 'Royal Purple').

Boutonnieres or corsages are traditionally given to the immediate family, the groomsmen, and the ushers. (Corsages are larger than boutonnieres and are generally constructed using more than one variety of flower or a group of two or three together with some leaves as backing.) Some couples also like to give each of their guests a flower as a symbol of their love and friendship—small, light flowers are best for this.

THIS PAGE By far the most popular choice of boutonniere is the white rose—here, *Rosa* 'Bianca' is shown embellished with a few *Eryngium planum* 'Blue Candle' thistles and dark green ivy. Other popular roses include the white 'Akito', pale gold 'Vendella', dark burgundy 'Black Baccara', bright red 'Grand Prix', lilac 'Cool Water', fuchsia pink 'Milano', or bright pink 'Barbie', lime green 'Emerald', yellow 'Taxi', and orange 'Milva'.

OPPOSITE A favorite wedding flower of mine is the Amazon lily *Eucharis amazonica*, which is the perfect combination of pure white petals and a lime-green center. Although Amazon lilies are available all the year round, this boutonniere for a winter wedding includes black privet berries and some lichen-covered larch twigs. ABOVE LEFT Orchids are a sensible choice for a boutonniere because they are long lasting. They are advisable if you are planning to get married at a hot time of year. ABOVE RIGHT *Cymbidium* 'Alice Anderson 49er' with a 'Vendela' rose edged with camellia leaves and ivy berries. BELOW A white moth orchid with New Zealand flax leaves and camellia alongside a *Cymbidium* 'R. B. Loes' with rosemary and *Senecio greyii*.

floral details

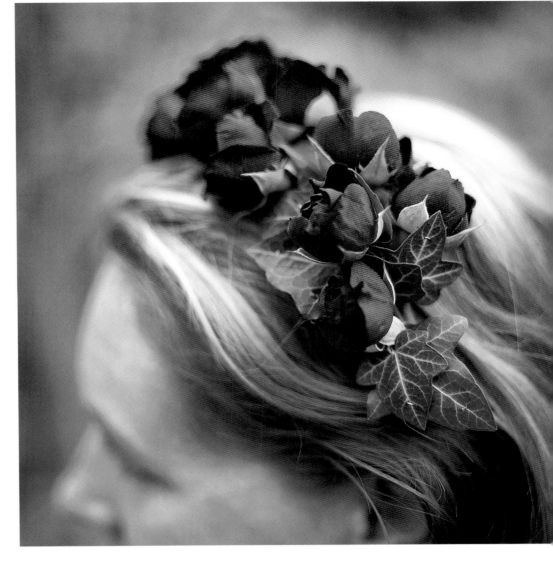

OPPOSITE A wrist corsage is an alternative way of accessorizing a bridesmaid or flower girl and is particularly suitable for the very young (or the very mature!) bridesmaid, who might not feel comfortable holding a bouquet. Currently wristlets, like these scented gardenias, are increasingly popular. **ABOVE** Wired rosebuds have been sewn onto a pair of ballet slippers to decorate a flower girl. If you wish to pin flowers onto your shoes or outfit, it is advisable to ask the florist to wire the blooms to make it easier to attach them. **RIGHT** Headbands are easier to wear than full circlets; here small 'Tamango' rose-buds have been wired and taped with dark green ivy leaves onto a plastic headband.

A talented florist will be able to make you any kind of floral accessory you require, from Cupid's bow and arrow to a halo for a cherubic bridesmaid. In the past, we have been asked to accessorize shoes, bridal gowns, handbags, hats, and even muffs. Your florist could create a pillow of flowers for your ring bearers, fashion a lucky horseshoe from white heather, sculpt a moss teddy bear for young bridesmaids, or design a floral crown to complete your veil. By the careful use of wired flower heads, many clever and intricate designs can be created to make your wedding truly individual.

ABOVE LEFT Round hoops or wreaths of flowers are an alternative way for your bridesmaids to carry flowers. Hydrangeas, peonies, calla lilies, roses, sweet peas, and Amazon lilies have been wired and taped onto a round metal frame. **ABOVE RIGHT** Singapore orchids (*Dendrobium*) have been individually wired and woven into a bridesmaid's hair. **RIGHT** Decorated prayer books were very fashionable for brides in the fifties and sixties, and this is still a pretty way of accessorizing books used for readings. Here hellebores, quince (*Chaenomeles japonica*), and spray roses have been wired together and tied to the book with raffia. **OPPOSITE** Offering a corsage or a boutonniere is a lovely way to welcome guests. Here the rare and unusual vanda orchid has been wired into a vibrant corsage. Orchids are my favorite flower for a corsage, because they are long-lasting and will still look good when the festivities are over.

how to make a rose pomander

Rose pomanders are popular for small bridesmaids, and they are a gorgeous floral accessory. They look particularly good when they are complementing rose nosegays, which are currently very popular. You can construct a pomander in many different ways, but the easiest method by far is to purchase a small ball of floral foam and attach a ribbon or cord. Then simply cut the roses with about ¾inch (2cm) of stem, and push them into the soaked ball all the way round. Although easy to construct in this way, soaked floral foam can be very heavy. The other downside to this type of pomander is that as the foam dries out some of the rose heads may become dislodged, and the pomander could start to break up.

The best method for making a pomander is to wire each rose head and place it into a ball of sphagnum moss. A simpler way is to use the method I have shown here, in which they are wired into a ball without any moss or foam. This is the lightest possible method for constructing a pomander. Traditionally, all bridal flowers were wired in this way, as it also makes the arrangement more secure and, therefore, much easier to hold. In recent years, there has been a preference for natural-looking flower decorations, and the more widespread use of floral foam has changed the way florists construct floral accessories. Wiring flowers in this way takes practice, and I do not recommend attempting to make a rose pomander for your own wedding without practicing several times first!

MATERIALS

40 roses (such as 'Vendela Rosita')
50 x 70 stub wires
50 x 28 silver wire
Gutta-percha tape
32 binding wire
Ribbon
Scissors
Nimble hands and lots of patience!

HOW TO

1 Cut off each rose head. Support each rose by placing a 70 stub wire up the middle of the stem and a 28 silver wire through the calyx to prevent it from twisting round on the stub wire. After you have wired and wire each flower head tape with gutta-percha tape.

2 Attach binding wire (32) to the first rose and start placing the rose heads together, binding around the wires as you go.

3 Build up the pomander by bending each rose to its position and binding as you go. Work round the pomander building up layers, and then working in towards the base.

4 When you have completed the pomander, and just before the last rose is in position, cut off any long wires and tape over the exposed ends. Wire in the ribbon at this end and then finish off by adding the last rose, taping it to the other stems with gutta-percha into the middle of the pomander. Reposition all the heads to make the top perfectly round, and mist with water to refresh the blooms, and make them last longer.

how to make a dog collar

Many couples want to include their pets in their special day and, now that a huge variety of ceremony sites is available, it is becoming far more common to include a dog—or even a horse—in the wedding celebrations. We have made several floral dog collars for our canine friends, as well as floral decorations for horse halters.

The easiest way to make a dog collar is to take a fabric collar and bind your flowers around this. If you can't find professional floral wires, you can create a very basic version by tying a few robust flower heads to some ivy vines and attaching these to the collar. For a more sophisticated version you will need a variety of heavy wires and some gutta-percha tape as well as some sturdy flowers. I prefer roses, hydrangeas, orchids, gerberas, *Amaranthus*, berries, and mixed foliage, but I have made them with delicate flower heads such as *Gloriosa* and ranunculus. (Here I have used 'Grand Prix' roses as they are lovely, sturdy, and strong.) The most important thing to do is to make sure that the floral collar is comfortable for your dog. The first thing he will do if he feels irritated is roll, and that will certainly crush the flowers. This is why I think the safest and best way to create an arrangement like this is to wire it onto to a collar that your dog is familiar with and that fits well. Once fitted, gently spruce up the flowers. Tell your dog how handsome/pretty he/she looks and instruct not to roll!

MATERIALS

12 roses (such as 'Grand Prix')
12 branches of skimmia foliage
3 large hydrangea heads.
Stub wires (0.90mm/20 guage and 0.71mm/22 guage) and silver wires (0.32mm/30 guage)
Gutta-percha tape
Scissors
A fabric dog collar

HOW TO

1 Cut off each flower head and add supporting wire. Wire each rose internally by inserting a 22-guage wire through the stem and into the calyx (the very base of the flower head). Add a silver wire through the calyx and secure it onto the main stem wire. Single-leg mount the skimmia with a 22-guage wire and the hydrangeas with a 30-guage silver wire. (Place one wire along the stem and wind the other leg over it three times.)

2 Tape with gutta-percha from the top of the wire to the bottom. This helps to protect the flower, keeping in moisture.

3 Measure one 20-guage wire around the dog's neck, to tape the flowers onto. Cover the wire with gutta-percha tape first to hide any joins.

4 Add the flowers and foliage, piece by piece, alternately using gutta-percha to secure; start at one end making a hook first. Cut off any unnecessary wires as you tape along. Finish the collar with another hook to act as a clasp, and secure it in place. Wire it onto the outside of the collar, adjust the fit, and talk sweetly to your dog!

the style of service

There is a well-known Chinese proverb that says that a journey of 10,000 miles begins with a single step. As you start to plan your wedding, you may be able to identify well with this. Making the initial and crucial decisions about the date, the site, and the timing can seem very daunting and more difficult than you expect. Whatever the location or timing, flowers are the perfect way of creating the right atmosphere and enhancing the ceremony, and with a little planning you'll find the perfect floral arrangement to suit your needs.

the site

Having set your date the next thing to do is to decide on the location and time of your ceremony. Traditionally the wedding was held close to bride's home, but if the bride and groom are arranging the wedding themselves, they may choose a place that is special or local to them, especially if the bride has been living away from home for many years.

The ceremony is the soul of the wedding, where you and your fiancé pledge your love for and loyalty to one another. Wherever you choose to hold your ceremony, there will, at some stage, be an exchange of vows, and this is the spiritual part of the day. The specifics of the ceremony will depend on your beliefs and preferences, and you may well have the opportunity to make this unique to you. Due to the immense range and style of wedding ceremonies, the choice of decoration also varies enormously. It may be that you have for a backdrop the hillside beside an English castle, a Venetian Palace and the Grand Canal, a chapel in Las Vegas, or a ruined church on a clifftop. Flowers will enhance any site. Whatever your religious preference and budget, there are certain ways that you can make a service more spiritual. The use of candles outside the site in hurricane lamps

or inside on stands adds ambiance. Even if you do not have a traditional place of worship you may wish to simulate an aisle or have your guests in a circle with you and your groom in the center.

Couples watching their costs may decide to forgo the expense of ceremony flowers and spend their resources on flowers for the reception, which will of course be enjoyed over a longer period. Alternatively, they may choose arrangements that they can take on to the reception and get the benefit of them for longer. There are limitations to this, as large flower arrangements do not travel well and you may require your florist to move them for you—this will incur added transport and labour costs on the day. For one outdoor wedding picnic, we arranged huge high-handled flower baskets containing scented stocks so that the guests could literally carry the decorations and the fragrance with them.

marrying outdoors

When planning an outdoor wedding it helps to think like an architect or a theater designer. Make sure that everyone can see and that there is adequate seating and protection from the elements. If you are on a limited budget, have one large arrangement on your altar or by the celebrant's table or, for a Jesish wedding, decorate only the top outside edges of the huppah.

One of the most effective outdoor wedding ceremonies I have seen had just one huge urn of pale pink hydrangeas and an aisle scattered with pale pink rose petals. The aisle was closed off with ribbon until the bride and her father arrived, so that the guests entered via the outer ends of the rows of chairs, making the rose-petalled path sacred to the bridal party. In civil ceremonies, flowers can be an important part of the proceedings, for example being offered to your new family. Sometimes roses are given to each of the parents, uniting the family in joyous celebration. This custom has its origins in Asia, where neck garlsnds are offered as a symbol of unity.

choosing your flowers

The color of your ceremony flowers may be determined by a number of influences. It may be the location you choose—if your ceremony is outdoors in the full summer sun then you may opt for brightly colored flowers or rich colors that will stand up to the bleaching effect of bright sunlight. In a temperate climate, the popularity of the all-white garden is reflected in the frequent choice of white-and-green color schemes for wedding flowers; both trends are influenced by a need to work with lower light levels. White and lime green are quite luminous together and work well in dark churches.

Apart from the light and the weather conditions, traditional or cultural beliefs may inspire your wedding color choice. In China, red and fuchsia are lucky and are the colors of marriage and good fortune. The luck associated with the humble shamrock in Ireland makes green the color of good luck and fertility. In India, where color is essential in the Hindu religion, brides are sprinkled with yellow turmeric; yellow and gold clothes are worn; and even yellow food is eaten to bring good fortune and health to the bride and groom. Or the color you choose may be distinctly personal—you may think of red as the color of love—or you may just select your favourite color to make you day special.

OPPOSITE Formal photography has been less popular recently as more couples have chosen to have reportage-style photographs. Although this large group, photographed outside St. Paul's Cathedral, in London, will have taken some time to organize, it's a good way of making sure you've got a picture of everyone who came to the wedding. RIGHT Ask your photographer to take some pictures of the ceremony site before the guests arrive, so that you've got a good record of how your flowers looked on the day—you will undoubtedly be too busy to do this later.

flowers in a church

Many churches can be magnificent buildings in themselves, and a few well-chosen flowers will increase the sense of occasion and pleasure. The flowers do not have to be costly or elaborate; a few pitchers of scented blooms in a small country church can look charming. If you have a limited budget, when planning the decoration for a medium-sized church it is better to have one or two major displays, rather than lots of small arrangements dotted around the place which will tend to get lost in their surroundings.

The larger the church, the more important the scale of any flower arrangement you include is, so if you are planning to hold your nuptials in a cathedral, think grand! If you really want to go to town and have a very flowery ceremony, then list all the places you would like flowers and see what fits the budget. It is especially welcoming to greet the guests with flowers at the entrance. Some churchyards have metal archways across gates where flowers can be attached, or swags can easily be attached to the gates themselves. The doorway to the church is a great place to construct an arch of flowers, which then becomes a fantastic frame for the photographs. But if the budget will not stretch that far, place some small flower arrangements in the alcoves to welcome the guests inside or topiary trees on either side of the door.

BELOW In Jewish weddings the ceremony takes place under a special canopy known as a huppah. Here a cream canopy has been decorated with four floral swags which have been tied to each of the posts. A huppah is set up on the morning of the wedding and is not a fixture of a synagogue. This means your florist will have to arrange your flowers on the morning of the wedding, not before.

Once inside the church, the focus for flowers should, I think, be the altar. Depending on the size of the church, it is good to have one or two large groupings of flowers here on tall pedestals. Remember that most of the service takes place between the pulpit and the lectern at the chancel rails. If the budget allows, my next priority is for small arrangements on every other pew if the furniture suits this and, if it does not, I like to add candle stands to frame the aisle. The aisle is the focus of attention for the processional, when the bride arrives and the recessional, when the newly married couple lead their guests from the church, and so is one of my favorite places to decorate. Of course there are many other possibilities, such as flowers in the font and flower arrangements at the base of every window. The different architecture of individual churches will offer other ideas for decoration, from screens within the church to collars around each pillar. It is always lovely to have some sort of floral decoration actually on the altar, too, as this is where the happy couple finish their prayers before the recessional.

Most churches have a church flower arrangers of their own and you should have an opportunity well before the wedding to see what level of skill they have. Some churches have bands of very talented and enthusiastic flower arrangers, who can do wonders with a few flowers and are often very generous, cutting additional plant material from their garden. But others are very amateur and you may not want them for your decorations. For my own wedding, I wanted to have flowers simply everywhere and so I enlisted the support of the church flower arrangers as well as using professional florists for some of the key areas of the church. I was married when I was serving my apprenticeship as a florist, before I had my own business, and I have to say the church flower arrangers did a very beautiful job. I was lucky enough to marry my husband, Peter, in the same church where my parents were married and so it was lovely to work with local people we had known for a long time. Whatever your situation, you will need to find out who is in charge of the flowers, as some churches do not allow outside florists and have a preferred team to work with.

It is also prudent and polite to check if there are any areas where you cannot have flowers as individual clergymen have their own views. It is also a good idea to find out whether there is another wedding on your chosen day, as this may mean that you can share the costs of the flowers. Do remember if you are planning a wedding during Lent the pastor may restrict you to just bringing in flowers for your ceremony, as flowers are not generally displayed in churches during this time. Remember, too, that in Advent the church may have its own decorations, including a nativity scene.

The Christian calender may influence the color of flowers displayed in a church. For example, yellow and white flowers are traditionally arranged in Easter. The only other considerations that might affect your choice of color are the altar cloth and any carpet. It is customary and polite to leave the wedding flowers for the enjoyment of the congregation for the Sunday service.

jewish ceremonies Officiated by

a rabbi, Jewish weddings can take place almost anywhere, so long as they are beneath a huppah. Some brides like to create their own huppah from tulle or embroidered fabric. Others ask florists to create an arbor or floral canopy, and these types can be especially effective for outdoor weddings. Over the years I have had the pleasure and honor of making many different styles of huppah—from an iconic frame fashioned only from gardenias to a fantasy tulle huppah with pink roses and a rustic birchwood frame for a country wedding.

Because the canopy is not fixed and is only set up in a synagogue on the day of the wedding, it is advisable to use a professional to decorate this. Normally floral decorations are hung at the top of the four poles. Sometimes the poles are garlanded, and they are occasionally totally covered with more elaborate decorations. If the budget allows, two larger arrangements may be placed at the arc of the synagogue and a trailing decoration included for the bima, where the register is signed.

flowers for civil ceremonies A judge performs a civil ceremony,

and this can take place anywhere, except a place of worship. In some countries (like Britain), the area or place has to be licensed to hold such an event, but others (like the United States and Australia) are much more liberal about this, and you can get married wherever you like. Civil ceremonies can be

ABOVE (CLOCKWISE FROM TOP LEFT) This traditional white-and-green arrangement in a formal verdigris urn is perfect for a simple church service; Garlands for columns are time-consuming to create and will require a site visit by your florist. This white-and-green garland with a Caribbean theme has been created by attaching floral foam cages to the top of the column and then arranging the flowers all around; Scattering petals to mark out the route for the bride is a fragrant and pretty way to start the ceremony.

just as spiritual and moving as religious ones, of course, and they can be more personal, as in some cases you have the freedom to write your own vows rather than be restricted to a prescribed wording.

The higher the ceiling in the ceremony building, the grander any flower arrangements need to be, especially in terms of their height, in order to make an impression. It is better to have one grand arrangement in a large space than ten small insignificant ones. It is always tempting to want an abundance of flowers all over the place, but always consider how the room will look when filled with people. One single, large arrangement that can be seen by everyone will say a lot more.

sculptural style

classic white flowers were given a contemporary twist for Natalie and Dariush's early spring wedding. Natalie chose to marry at home, and so a large marquée was constructed in the garden of her parents' home. A Persian ceremony at home was followed by a Catholic blessing in the family church, then champagne and canapés were served in the garden before the wedding breakfast in the marquee. To complement her off-the-shoulder dress, Natalie chose a dome of roses edged with dark green aspidistra leaves.

The flowers for both ceremonies were full of white spring blossoms, including cherry blossom, spiraea, and lilac, massed with ranunculus, stocks, lilies, and roses. Natalie's attendants carried a mixture of blooms to continue the theme. Her chief bridesmaid carried a bouquet of lily-of-the-valley and roses. (Spring is the best and least expensive time for lily-of-the-valley as it is in season). Her younger bridesmaids carried white sweet peas edged with guelder rose and galax leaves. The delightful flower girl carried a small nosegay of lily-of-the-valley. All the bridesmaids wore individually wired hair adornments, so that the hairdressers could pin them easily into their hair. The groomsmen wore rose boutonnieres with a star-shaped head of Persian tuberose. A pale silver fabric was chosen for the tables in the marquee, creating a very cool, chic look. As Natalie had a large wedding (with over two hundred guests), she chose to have five

ABOVE Natalie and Dariush on the way to church following their Persian ceremony. Natalie chose white 'Akito' roses in a neat rose dome, edged with folded aspidistra leaves. Dariush's buttonhole is, of course, a single 'Akito' rose. **BELOW LEFT** Natalie and Dariush beneath the canopy at the Persian ceremony. The room is decorated with masses of Persian tuberose and jasmine, creating a wonderful sweet scent. Huge vases are filled with calla lilies, blossoms and guelder roses and edged with the arched spring greens of Solomon's seal. The white-and-green theme creates a coolly sophisticated look.

different table designs spread across the marquee, resulting in flowers at different heights spread out across the site. She chose sophisticated flowers, including amaryllis, orchids, and calla lilies, which were combined with roses to create a very sculptured and very contemporary look.

The horseshoe-shaped top table was raised on a platform and decorated with tall vases topped with moth orchids and pots of lily-of-the-valley. The tallest table arrangements were moth orchids and calla lilies. Amaryllis trees made medium-height displays, and cubes filled with plaited flax leaves, roses, and cymbidium orchids created a third, lower display. Finally, glass dishes were filled with the green 'Midori' *Anthurium*, papyrus, and calla lilies. The tables were all decorated with candles surrounded by *Equisetum* and votives. Napkin ties of flax and orchids for some tables and stephanotis vines and florets for the others created a very lush table setting for each of the guests. After the wedding breakfast, the dancing began and all the candles and votives were lit. Many more candles and votive lights were placed on pedestals around the edge, and the star cloth above the dance floor created the perfect ambiance for dancing under the stars!

ABOVE For the marquee, Natalie chose a mixture of tall, medium, and low arrangements, as well as using glass dishes filled with flowers, breaking up the expanse of the marquee. The combination of orchids and calla lilies brings a striking and contemporary look to the blank canvas of the marquee. RIGHT A four-tiered stand of champagne glasses, topped with an elegant arrangement of flowers and foliage, awaits the start of the festivities. BELOW LEFT The top table is a horseshoe shape and is raised on a platform, so that all the guests can see the bride and groom. It is decorated with masses of stephanotis vines and tall glass vases topped with moth orchids. Pots massed with lily-of-the-valley are dotted along the top table. BELOW RIGHT The three-tiered cake is decorated with sugar calla lilies and surrounded by *Equisitum* tanks filled with rose domes. The table is edged with stephanotis vines.

decorating the site

Although you are in the ceremony for only a very short time, it is essentially the heart of the wedding. Flowers will be the most significant way you can personalize the space and create an ambiance. If you decide on a religious ceremony, you will have to check with the priest, rabbi, or minister as to what decorations are allowed. If you choose to have a civil ceremony, it is likely that you may need a slightly larger budget for your flowers as you will be creating your own special atmosphere. Many traditional religious venues are beautiful and highly decorative and therefore require less decoration.

LEFT It has become customary to adorn a huppah by decorating the four poles. Here floral foam cages have been attached to the front and back of the pole so that flowers can be arranged on the inside and the outside of the canopy. Trails of jasmine have been added to trail the length of the pole and provide scent for the bridal party. **ABOVE** Ceremony flowers are best displayed on stands which make the flowers easily visible. Here a glass urn of late summer flowers sits on a silver leaf pedestal. The choice of flowers for a large arrangement should be bold, big heads, such as hydrangeas and chrysanthemums, with spires of *Molucella* and delphinium and trails of lisianthus and *Amaranthus*. **OPPOSITE** A loose arrangement of spring blossoms, early tree foliage such as *Sorbus*, and white delphiniums and lilies make a lovely scented vase to welcome your guests.

OPPOSITE With a small church, it is possible to decorate nearly all the windows and also the Lady Chapel. Here a trailing arrangement of lilies has been placed in the center of the window, with votive lights surrounding it. It is customary to use the appropriate vases that belong to the church for altar arrangements.
ABOVE LEFT A trailing table arrangement of bright red gerberas, cymbidium orchids, *Alpinia*, *Molucella* and *Howea* palm leaves makes a perfectly shaped display for the registrar's table at a civil ceremony. Often this kind of trailing arrangement can then be moved onto the top table if you have a linear arrangement. **ABOVE RIGHT** A classic pedestal arranged for a wedding at a country house using vibrant red *Heliconia*, *Alpinia*, 'Grand Prix' roses, *Molucella*, trailing *Amaranthus*, and lots of lush tropical foliage.
RIGHT Candlelight adds to the romance of any kind of ceremony. Decorations like these can always be moved on to the reception after the ceremony for maximum use.

chairbacks

Wherever possible, I like my flower arrangements to look very natural, and so the design of a simple swag of flowers for a pew or chair is, for me, one of the most effective ways of making a site look pretty, whether it is for the ceremony or the reception. We very often move the chairbacks that have been used for the ceremony to the reception venue and then tie them on to the chairs for the top table.

LEFT A few stems of the unusual purple vanda orchid have been tied together with some curled aspidistra leaves and a bundle of fresh bamboo to create a chairback with an Oriental theme. **ABOVE LEFT** Simple tied nosegays of garden roses attached to a banqueting chair are a lovely way of marking out an aisle for a country wedding. **ABOVE** Slipcovers are a smart way of theming a wedding; flowers can still be attached to the back by using a thick white cord. Here calla lilies and *Anthurium* have been mixed with *Phormium* and date palm for a tropical arrangement. **OPPOSITE** *Fatsia* leaves make the perfect background for *Agapanthus* and roses, which are tied onto some antique Venetian chairs for a romantic wedding in Venice.

how to make a **chairback**

A chairback is essentially a tied swag of flowers which usually includes foliage. I love to incorporate these into my weddings, as they are very pretty and add an informal touch to a ceremony. They are quite easy to make, especially if you use only one type of flower, such as gerbera, daisies, or roses.

For a pew end decoration or for a chairback for the center of a chair, you do need more skill to get a flat back to the display and a lovely elevated diamond shape for the flowers to look really good. The secret to success is choosing the right foliage and flowers. I normally use at least five types of foliage. You need something flat for the back like a branch of camellia, beech, laurel, or a large leaf like *Monstera*. I like to add some textural foliage such as *Hypericum* berries, poppy seed heads, or rose hips, and some fluffy foliage like *Alchemilla mollis*, grasses, or branches of flower blossom in the spring time. Add a selection of pointed or long flowers such as calla lilies, roses, *Lysimachia*, and veronica and use round larger-headed flowers such as gerbera germini, open roses, dahlias, or achillea, as well as some trailing blooms, like lisianthus or amaranthus. Once you have made your decision on the choice of flowers, it is essential to clear any excess foliage from below the binding point. (This is where you hold the hand tie while making it and it becomes the tie point when completed.) It may help you to lay the flowers out in their groups before you start, to make it easier as you build the swag.

MATERIALS

Mango calla lilies
Millet grass
Achillea
Confetti roses
Salal
Hypericum
Ivy
Hydrangea
A length of tie and ribbon
Scissors

HOW TO

1 First arrange your foliage, starting with the flat leaves at the back and adding more interesting textural foliage at the front, to make a diamond shape. Feed some of the berries through to create some elevation to the swag.

2 Starting with the calla lilies, place one towards the top of the hand tie to make the point of the swag. Feed in other flowers at different heights within the design, alternating from left to right.

3 Add the roses and *achillea* in the same way, pulling them down to graduate through the swag. Spiral the stems in the binding point to create a neat hand tie. The flowers will be shorter towards the binding point, but try to leave them long enough to stand proud and not appear squashed. The largest flowers should be the most noticeable and in the best position.

4 Attach the swag to the chair with a strong wire cord or binding wire, and then make a three-looped bow to cover the binding point.

how to make a heart wreath

A simple heart wreath is a lovely way to accessorize a door or a gate for your wedding, and because it is made using a wet floral foam frame it can be made a few days in advance of your special day. One of these would look great on a church door or gates, or at the entrance to your ceremony. Occasionally, we create these for the bride's home to welcome her guests. Roses and orchids are excellent for this design, because they last a long time and have regular shapes, but you could use hydrangeas for a fall wedding, ranunculus for spring, and sweet peas for the summer. When you are choosing the flowers and foliage for this wreath, look for colors that enhance each other. Here I chose the 'Black Baccara' roses because their color coordinated so perfectly with the burgundy nose of the cymbidium orchid, and I chose skimmia foliage because it matches the rest of the scheme.

The ribbons from which the wreath is suspended are deliberately narrow so that they don't overwhelm the bouquet, but you might choose to have a wider, more substantial ribbon or a selection of different colored narrow ones to add something a little extra. Alternatively, if there is a strong and large enough hook on the place where you want to hang the finished wreath, you needn't worry about the ribbon at all. It is always worth considering how you are going to hang your wreath before you start decorating it, because the position of the hook might affect how much ribbon you need.

MATERIALS

1 x 18-inch (45-cm) wide floral foam heart
1 knife
36 inch (90 cm) of ½-inch (12-mm) red ribbon
Galax leaves
25 stems of red skimmia foliage
25 stems of large headed cymbidium orchids
60 'Black Baccara' roses
Floristry scissors or secateurs

HOW TO

1 Soak the floral foam heart in a large basin for a few minutes until the bubbles cease to rise. Use the knife to trim the edge of the foam, so that you can place the flower heads more easily to achieve a rounded shape. Fold the ribbon in half and tie the loose ends securely around the top of the heart.

2 Push the galax leaves into the foam around the outside edge and then across the front, so that they are slightly overlapping each other.

3 Fill the front and sides of the heart wreath with the skimmia, which forms the base for the flowers. Cut each piece into lengths of 1¼–2 inch (3–5 cm) and then scatter evenly between the galax leaves. Position the orchids evenly around the wreath.

4 Finally carefully slot in the roses, filling the gaps between the cymbidium orchids and ensuring that you reflect the heart shape of the foam when positioning each one. When finished, mist the wreath and keep it in a cool place until you are ready to hang it.

the **main** event

For most couples, the reception is the party of a lifetime. It celebrates their marriage and marks the culmination of many months of planning. They want the reception to be unforgettable, to bring them together with their loved ones, and to unite two sets of friends. When it comes to the floral decoration, the possibilities are endless, and, whatever the budget you are working to, it's possible to create a memorable and imaginative reception.

planning your reception

Your reception can be as unique as you want to make it—from an early wedding and a superb simple brunch to a late afternoon wedding or a lavish and elegant dinner dance. Most people go for the middle of the day and have an afternoon reception. Certainly limiting the length of your reception will help to curtail the expense. One option is to have an afternoon tea reception. Instead of large round tables, you can hire smaller ones and use fewer table decorations and simple flowers for the table or even choose one striking plant such as an exotic orchid.

Traditionally the wedding reception was held in the bride's family home. Over time this tradition has prevailed and it is still lovely to have a home wedding, if practical. You do need to have adequate space, though, and a home reception is a lot more effort and work for all members of the family. Providing services such as adaquate toilets and parking can become a logistical nightmare and cause tempers to be frayed. Over the years, it became more common to hold the reception in a local hotel or hall, but more recently there has been a trend

ABOVE Long narrow tables need linear style arrangements. This summer arrangement was created using a flat tray, floral foam, and a mixture of pale pink peonies, purple sweet peas, sky-blue delphiniums, bright pink ranunculuses, white *Philadelphus*, and sprays of lime-green *Viburnum opulus*.

away from traditional sites towards informal and varied locations—museums, mansions, even zoos! But whatever your choice of site the three basic elements that contribute towards a successful and enjoyable reception are the decorations, catering, and the entertainment.

the florist's role
For the decorations, most florists today offer more than just flowers. Many can also advise you on the look of the tables, including details such as renting tablecloths, chairs, and seat covers to help you to create the ambiance you have in mind. Florists work so frequently with caterers and other related industries that they can often be a great source of recommendation as to whom to call for an estimate and whom they enjoy working with. Florists will often work closely with the caterers in particular to confer on the canapé decorations, and to design the floral decorations for the buffet. Often they will meet with you at your tasting to discuss the food and table decorations in more detail. They also liaise with cake decorators to ensure that the cake table perfectly complements the room.

A creative florist will meet you at your chosen site and will give you the best advice on where to place flowers and how many you should ideally have. Most often, florists advise their clients to have fewer, rather than more, flowers but to go for grander displays which will be more striking when the party begins and the room begins to fill with guests. You also need to consider the installation and setting up of the room and the timings for this. Hotels may have more than one reception in a day, so you will be allocated a particular time slot that must be rigidly adhered to, or rented spaces may limit access times for your deliveries and services.

A florist's mission is to take your chosen reception site and change it into a room that is special and has the correct ambience for your wedding day. The blander the room, the more you will need to spend on the decorations, so think seriously about this when looking at your

budget. Often a more expensive site needs a lot less decoration and this can, in the long run, work out cheaper. Really formal sites do, however, necessitate huge and costly arrangements. Unusual sites may be more complicated for your contractors to work in. Stately homes and museums often limit the hours of parking and may be open to the public for part of the day, making the lead time for your caterer and florist very limited! If this is the case, it may mean that your florist does not have much time for complicated on-site arrangements, and everything may have to be completed off site and positioned quickly.

Fragrance is very important at the reception. I think that it is essential to have some scented flowers, incense, or scented candles at the entrance for your greeting line or cocktail hour. This is so evocative and the scents will always remind you of your special day. Don't forget to

ABOVE (CLOCKWISE FROM TOP LEFT)
Herbs are lovely to include in your wedding reception for their scent. Here rosemary has been attached to a glass tumbler, using double-coated tape to make a pretty, scented candleholder; A floral wreath for your door or entrance is a dramatic way of welcoming your guests to the reception. This wreath has been created using hydrangeas and white garden roses on a foam ring. Keep wreaths such as this cool and mist with water until you are ready to put them in place; A glass cube vase of white Avalanche roses filled with limes and edged with ostrich feathers makes a striking contemporary arrangement.

check out the rest rooms, and add some lovely touches such as flowers and scented votives to make your guests feel pampered.

creating your theme
My favorite sites to decorate are marquees or tented receptions because they offer the florist a blank canvas to work on, but any room can be transformed to fit any theme with a little imagination and a lot of money! For example, one hotel ballroom was transformed into a Moroccan palace with a club feel using brightly colored fabric, a tented roof, and swags of tiny "pea" lights. Incense and fragrant flowers helped to set the scene further. On another occasion, to create a gypsy theme, pieces of mirror glass were sewn on tablecloths of intense color. A roving gypsy-style musical group worked the room and the flowers were jewel colored throughout.

If your room is very decorative to start with lavish floral decorations may compete too much. Often the best schemes are monochromatic colors of cream and white flowers. This may seem like the obvious route to take, but it does work very well and that is a reason for its endurance as a theme. It is classic and very beautiful. It can be made to look striking and minimal or romantic and blowsy. Fruit can also make a monochromic display more striking and add interest.

lighting
Your florist will also advise you on lighting—whether it be the addition of candelabras or votives to the table or getting an estimate for a party lighting expert for making the best of your decorations. I cannot emphasize too strongly how important this is—the whole ambiance of the wedding is determined by how comfortable and attractive the lighting is. Most ballrooms or spaces of a similar size have lighting that can be dimmed, and each centerpiece can be spotlit from the ceiling, which greatly enhances the floral arrangements. Candlelight is flattering, and the right lighting level makes everyone feel more confident and relaxed. If you decide to appoint a lighting company, there are no limits as to what can be achieved, from uplighting floral arrangements to huge flambeaux for the entrance and a dramatic firework display for the finale. You will have an engineer on site all night to highlight your special moments, such as the cutting of the cake and the first dance. You may even choose to project images or stars and moons or decide to change the color of the room through the use of light gels. Often these companies can also provide amplification systems if you are planning a large event.

chairbacks
Chairs are an important consideration too because there are so many of them in the room, and generally there are very few designs—rental chairs are the same all over the world! It is a good idea to personalize at least the top table using chairback arrangements, tiny garlands of flowers, or even a simple bow.

centerpieces
The practice of adorning tables with flowers, herbs, and petals dates as far back as ancient Greece and Romem and has endured to the present day. The newlyweds' table, whether it be formal or round, should be different and more opulent to differentiate the bride and groom from their guests. If you are having a large wedding, with over 200 guests, you may consider having some tall table arrangements to make the most of your space. It is currently very popular to

BELOW A favourite design for an autumnal wedding reception using waxy deep red apples wired into a basket around a plastic dish filled with foam and then topped with dahlias, 'Grand Prix' and 'Milva' roses, rosehips, berries, skimmia and crocosmia. Alternatively for a white-and-green theme you could use 'Granny Smith' apples or use oranges to bring a vibrant color to the table.

have a mixture of half the tables set with tall arrangements, and the other half low ones. If you are planning 300 guests you may even have three heights of arrangements. Tall arrangements are usually candelabras, topiary trees, or tall glass vases so the flowers are raised above the table. Usually a florist tries to raise these above the heads of the diners, and the thin stem of the candelabra, tree, or vase allows guests to see each other across the table. It is very difficult to hold a conversation with guests sitting directly opposite you on a round table, because such tables are normally 5 to 6 feet (1.5 to 2 metres) across

and the ambiant noise precludes this activity, but it is always more comfortable to be able to at least see across the table, so bear this in mind when discussing the table flowers with your florist.

decorating the table Table linen is very important. Most hotels offer

white as standard, but all caterers can hire in linen of many colors and shades. Standard colors and sizes are less expensive than cloths that fall to the floor in deep or rich colors. Personally, I prefer tablecloths to reach the floor. Your florist can help you choose a color that complements your flowers and may even rent the linen for you. Napkins are a similar consideration. You can have them trimmed with taffeta ribbon, make them into a folded bed for an orchid, or even use a sprig of herbs to decorate them and to scent your tables. Place cards are normally coordinated with the linen and flowers, as are the menu cards. Your florist and caterer will be able to recommend a calligrapher to help with these if necessary.

ABOVE (CLOCKWISE FROM TOP LEFT) Scattering rose petals onto a table is a romantic idea; An autumnal arrangement uses tomato eggplant (*Solanum integrifolium*) with black berries and lime-green balls of *Aschlepias physocarpa* in strong bands and topped with six savoy cabbages filled with confetti roses; A simple stacked cake, baked by the bride herself, has been decorated with flower heads and a small arrangement of flowers, which has been created in the bottom part of a white polystyrene cup. The bridal bouquet of lily-of-the-valley, *Alchemilla mollis*, and garden roses has sensibly been placed back into a vase during the reception.

the wedding cake The cake is the centerpiece of

the reception and another area where you can let your imagination run wild, commissioning any design. In the United States, it is common to have two cakes: the traditional white wedding cake and the groom's cake, usually chocolate but sometimes a fruit cake. Often the choice is left to the groom, and this is a lovely way of including him in the arrangements. It is also a clever way of offering two cake options. The cutting of the cake normally happens towards the end of the reception; the bride takes the knife and the groom puts his hand on hers. A wish accompanies this and then traditionally they feed one another!

sophisticated city chic

a spectacular ballroom was the setting for Annabel and Stephen's wedding reception, after a ceremony at the historic Bevis Marks Synagogue. They shared the floral decorations for the synagogue with another bride and groom, who were marrying before them, so I did not have the pleasure of arranging the flowers for their ceremony. I did organize the flowers for the reception, however. Annabel and her family chose a lime green, bright pink, and lilac theme for the wedding, and so a very romantic collection of flowers was chosen for the centerpieces and large arrangements. Annabel wore a delicious gold gown, and she wanted to hold a simple hand-tied shower of orchids. To accommodate her wish, we were able to order a rare orchid from our specialist grower, which complemented the color of her gown perfectly.

Because a ballroom is so large, it suits flower arrangements at several heights, including some tall designs to fill the space. All the arrangements included candles and masses of votives on the tables. The tall arrangements were placed in simple zinc stands adorned with crystals to match the magnificent chandeliers. The single candlesticks also sported dropped crystals, making the tall tables very sparkly. The tall arrangements were created by using roses and hydrangeas in pink, lilac, and green. The long, trailing green plant is *Amaranthus*, which creates a lovely sumptuous effect in tall arrangements such as these. The stem of the stand is thin so that guests can still see across the table and enjoy each other's company, although it is usually quite difficult to talk across a table of twelve in a large ballroom! The medium-height arrangements were full mounds of roses, hydrangeas, and lisianthus in lilacs and lime greens, with a shot of bright pink. The low arrangements were floral rings encircling large glass bowls filled with lilac floating candles. Lilac candles were used throughout the ballroom, and each napkin was tied with a navy bow to match the cupels used in the wedding ceremony. The men's napkins were decorated with a sprig of rosemary while the ladies had a 'Blue Gene' rose as well as rosemary.

ABOVE The bride and groom share a moment on their own. Annabel's hand-tied shower bouquet features moth orchids, chosen specifically to match her golden gown. **RIGHT** The three styles of arrangement in the magnificent ballroom at the hotel. Grand rooms like this benefit from arrangements of varying heights to break up the space. Matching candles, tablecloth, and napkin decorations complete the look.

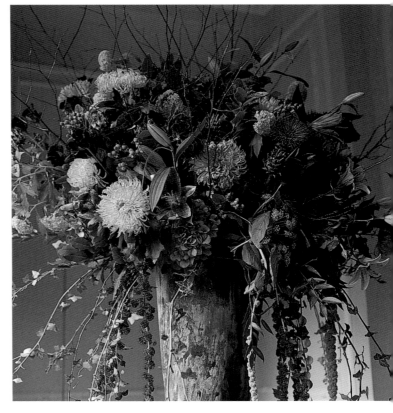

ABOVE LEFT A few splashes of rain did not dampen the spirits of the bride and groom as—just married—they leave the synagogue for their reception. **ABOVE RIGHT** The side table is flanked with white moth orchids and Italian papyrus grass in a tall lily vase. **RIGHT** This huge pedestal was created using many late summer blooms in pink, lime greens, and lilacs. Bright pink 'Milano' roses and 'Medusa' lilies look fabulous with the spiky standard lime green chrysanthemums and big lilac ornamental cabbages. The trailing red flower is *Amaranthus*, mixed with the green variety and lots of trailing ivies. **BELOW** The ladies' napkins are trimmed with a rose and a sprig of rosemary and tied with a navy bow.

"Our day was simply perfect. Paula worked her magic and the site looked spectacular."
ANNABEL

OPPOSITE Stemmed glass bowls have been lined with leaves and filled with flowers in the same pink, lilac, and green theme. They are encircled by four tall lilac candles. TOP LEFT Individual cup cakes decorated with a lilac sugar rose were displayed on five tiers of glass and decorated with real lilac roses and rosemary. ABOVE, LEFT One of the tall arrangements —featuring roses and hydrangeas in pink, lilac, and green. Trailing strands of amaranthus balance the height of the arrangement, and the thin-stemmed stand doesn't obstruct the guests' view across the table. ABOVE, RIGHT The bride and groom stop for a photo in front of one of the large pedestal arrangements. LEFT Straight-sided glass bowls are edged with a floral foam ring and then filled with foliage and groups of roses and hydrangeas. Lilac candles float on the water to give a sparkly effect. BELOW The napkins for the male guests are trimmed with a sprig of rosemary and tied with a navy satin bow to match their cupels.

centerpieces

As food is the center of any reception, it is inevitable that your table will be the focus of the evening and your center-pieces of paramount importance. Floral arrangements can be tall, low, or differing heights, depending on the size of your site. You can use candelabras, topiary trees, or vases and bowls, and votive candles can be incorporated into your centerpiece design. Flowers bring luxury, beauty, and fragrance to the table.

OPPOSITE FAR LEFT A simple centerpiece to recreate at home uses a savoy cabbage as the base for arranging half a dozen "Iceberg" roses. **OPPOSITE, TOP** A red square box and four tapered red candles are the basis for this contemporary arrangement, which uses nuts and flowers in compact groups. **OPPOSITE, BOTTOM** This winter arrangement has been designed on a square ceramic dish and includes three frosted pale pink candles and six waxed and frosted pears. The delicate Easter lily has been mixed with tuberose and grey foliage (*Senecio*) and a South African foliage called *Brunia albiflora*. **THIS PAGE** A vibrant lime-green and red theme was used throughout this autumnal wedding. This hand-tied bouquet is of ivy, red germini gerberas, 'Grand Prix' roses, and cymbidium orchids.

OPPOSITE I prefer savoy cabbages as decoration, rather than to eat, because of their glaucous green color which seems to complement any flower. They are also very textural, and just by adding one or two roses, you can make something that is quite simple look quite grand. **THIS PAGE** Another favorite centerpiece (which I use a lot in my own home because it is simple to create) features floating candles. Three different-height cylinders each contain one giant floating candle and are surrounded by a large floral foam wreath, filled with autumnal flowers, berries, and apples, and encircled by votives.

THIS PAGE Flax (*Phormium*) leaves have been woven to create a basket-like effect inside a low glass cube vase. Calla lilies, cymbidium orchids, date palm, and tropical leaves are arranged inside it for a table in a smart private dining room. The original inspiration for weaving leaves in this way came from a trip to Thailand. **OPPOSITE** Three giant fish bowls have been filled with yellow calla lilies (*Zantedeschia* 'Florex Gold'), with a tiny amount of water in each, and then stacked on top of one another. This design works well with linear flowers such as tulips, moth orchids, and climbing lilies.

THIS PAGE, ABOVE AND LEFT The dark wood interior of the synagogue is enhanced with white and green spring blooms. The historic pews in the front rows are too delicate to sit on and so are decorated with garlands of ivy and groups of white 'Bianca' roses. Candlelight and traditional arrangements complemented the site perfectly. **OPPOSITE, FAR RIGHT** Keren and Daniel preparing for their official photographs in a London garden square. Keren wore an elegant strapless dress, with a small bolero added for the ceremony because it is not considered appropriate to have bare arms in a synagogue. **OPPOSITE, TOP** Keren carried a round wired bouquet of stephanotis florets with some trails and edged with camellia leaves. **OPPOSITE, BOTTOM** Keren's beautiful dress was designed by London wedding gown designer, Ritva Westinius.

from traditional to modern

taking a different approach for the ceremony and the reception made the early February wedding of Keren to Daniel an extremely beautiful and elegant affair. Traditional decoration in the synagogue contrasted with cool contemporary arrangements in a local hotel, where the wedding party feasted and danced the night away. Keren had a clear idea when we first met that she wanted the flowers to be white and green, architectural, striking, and modern for the reception, and those for the ceremony to be softer and traditional. The synagogue is a beautiful candlelit site and we filled it with early white and green spring blossoms such as lilac, *Viburnum opulus*, *Prunus*, *Euphorbia fulgens*, jasmine, and scented lilies. Jewish weddings are conducted under a canopy, and it has become the custom to decorate the four corners with hanging swags or garlands of flowers and foliage. This is best done on site where you can position the floral foam and then arrange the foliage and flowers around the pole. Since the canopy is set up on the morning of the wedding, the flowers are very fresh. The white and green perfectly complemented the simplicity of the building and were very fragrant. When the candles were lit, the ceremony looked truly magical.

For the reception, Keren decided on "living topiaries" of white amaryllis on huge glass dishes, with large tropical leaves and textural seed heads for half of the tables. For the others, she chose very tall fluted vases filled to the ceiling with extra-tall papyrus from Italy and sprays of white moth orchids and *Anthurium* 'Midori'. The use of two heights of table decorations for a ballroom gives height to the room while allowing the guests to see across the table. Masses of frosted glass votives encircled the arrangements, and each guest was given

a cymbidium orchid head, which was tucked into their napkin. The bride and groom sat at a table for two, with tables for their respective families on either side, and the table was decorated with a trailing arrangement of *Euphorbia* and orchids. *Monstera* leaves decorated the card table and a huge working fountain was placed in the foyer and decorated with orchids to welcome the guests. The buffet tables were decorated with glass vases filled with Brussels sprouts and savoy cabbages filled with roses and orchids. The arrangements throughout the reception site were contemporary, using large glass vases and pedestals of clear plastic, filled with pussy willow and blossom.

"It could not have been more perfect and magical." KEREN

OPPOSITE (CLOCKWISE FROM TOP LEFT) Open amaryllis (*Hippeastrum* 'Mont Blanc') are tied together at the base of their flower heads to create a living topiary; A tall flared vase is lined with horsetail (*Equisetum*) and filled with cymbidium orchids and blossom; Low, trailing table arrangements are perfect for top tables, as they create a lovely frame for photographs; A delicate cymbidium orchid is tucked into each guest's napkin. THIS PAGE, ABOVE The two heights of table arrangements—amaryllis trees and taller glass flutes filled with moth orchids. LEFT A sushi bar is decorated with a large glass vase filled with brussels sprouts and savoy cabbages and topped with roses, cabbages, and cymbidium orchids. BELOW A clear plastic dish has been filled with a glass globe, bunches of pussy willow, and two large balls of amaryllis.

table settings

However large or small your wedding, you will require some decoration on the tables. This can be as simple as a lovely plant, such as a marguerite, with its pot wrapped in muslin, or a seasonal chrysanthemum in a basket. For a slightly higher budget, you can choose a simple tied bunch of seasonal flowers, such as daffodils or tulips in spring, cornflowers in summer, dahlias or zinnias for autumn, or berries and foliage for winter.

OPPOSITE Horsetail (*Equisitum*) has been glued together to make a natural napkin ring. **THIS PAGE** A rose ('Xtreme') mixed with elder berries, ivy berries, skimmia, and oak leaf has been arranged in a water phial covered with an aspidistra leaf and tied with sea grass, as a fresh floral favor.

OPPOSITE Cube vases are the most versatile vase for table decorations. Filled with cranberries and topped with 'Grand Prix' roses, red cotoneaster berries, gerbera 'Chateau', dark red *Amaranthus*, and skimmia, this monochromatic table centre is perfect for a fall wedding.

THIS PAGE By folding the napkin, you can create a pocket—the perfect place to insert an orchid head, such as this cymbidium orchid. In fall, small apples and pears that do not make the grade for human consumption are waxed and covered in glitter for decoration.

OPPOSITE A climbing lily has been tied to a napkin with a mousseline bow. The inscription on the ribbon is "The flower is a leaf mad with love" by the German philosopher Goethe. THIS PAGE Three yellow ranunculuses (my favorite flower) are tied with raffia for a simple but striking napkin decoration.

cakes

One of the highlights of the reception is, of course, the cutting of the cake. There are so many imaginative cake makers available that you really can have anything you desire from a multi-tiered selection of small cupcakes to a lavish five-tiered sugar-flowered design. The choice of flowers to decorate the cake is equally wide, and once you've agreed on a design, your florist will be able to advise you on the perfect floral embellishments.

OPPOSITE (CLOCKWISE FROM FAR LEFT) A pink-striped stacked cake has been decorated at the base with a ring of pink roses— 'Rosita Vendella', 'Dolce Vita', and 'Barbie'—and pink hydrangeas; Individual cakes have been simply decorated with a marguerite; A highly decorative cake with floral embroidery-style icing has been topped with a small trailing arrangement of pink and purple flowers to match. They are sweet peas (*Lathyrus odoratus*), *Lysimachia*, ranunculus, love-in-a-mist (nigella), *Leucocoryne* 'Caravelle', and trailing ivies. **THIS PAGE** A three-tiered square cake has been decorated with two tiers of multi-colored roses (the bright orange 'Narangar', the burgundy bi-color 'Ruby Red', the bright pink 'Milano', the golden 'Tresor 2000', and the burgundy 'Black Baccara') and a top box filled with lines of roses.

a touch of the romantic

just seven months after meeting her at a private gallery, Viorel visited Natalia in Barcelona and he proposed with a gorgeous classic ring from Tiffany. Natalia, originally from Russia, and Viorel, from Romania, wanted their respective backgrounds to be reflected in their wedding, so they began to plan a wedding with lots of traditional touches from their homelands. Natalia loved Tchaikovsky's *Swan Lake*, so that became the theme for their very romantic wedding. A mint-green feather was slipped into each of the wedding invitations, and ostrich-feather boas were used to decorate the flower arrangements. Her bridesmaid also wore mint green, and Viorel sported a mint-green cravat. Natalia chose to hold white calla lilies with an ostrich-feather collar, which looked amazing with her fairy tale gown. After their civil ceremony at a register office, the happy couple released a pair of white doves, which is a gesture of peace and love to celebrate the vows the couple had just exchanged. The doves fly away together, symbolizing the new union (and continuing Natalia's romantic bird theme). As most of their guests were visiting from overseas, Natalia and Viorel wanted to show them a little bit of the city, and so they hired traditional buses to take them all to a huge ferris wheel on the banks of a river, on which they had hired two private capsules. Here they all enjoyed champagne while admiring the panorama of the city streets below them.

The reception was held at Natalia's favourite site, a minimalist hotel—a large white space with the entrance filled with masses of moth phalaenopsis orchids. At first, the guests mingled in the gardens while sipping more champagne and listening to Tchaikovsky's *Swan Lake* played by a string quartet. They could also admire two huge ice sculptures of swans decorated with dendrobium orchids, pink calla lilies, and long *Ruscus* garlands that had been set into a square pond in the center of the garden. We had also decorated all the other ponds with floating orchid heads, and the iron arch over the gate that marked the entrance to the garden with white bougainvillea, pale pink moth orchids, and green trailing *Amaranthus*. Following drinks and Russian caviar in the hotel grounds, the guests went into the restaurant for dinner. Here, the black tablecloths were decorated with square vases filled with limes and white 'Iceberg' roses and encircled with white ostrich feathers. The minimalist interior of the hotel was the perfect backdrop for the bold contemporary theme. Each place card was attached to a single pink calla lily with a stem of *Dasylirion*. After dinner, the couple cut their swan-like white chocolate cake while a Russian gypsy band played. Following their first dance (a Russian waltz), the dancing began with a mixture of Russian and Romanian tunes, giving the reception a real Eastern-European flavor.

ABOVE Natalia and Viorel share a romantic moment outside the register office. Viorel's calla lily boutonniere matches Natalia's bouquet. His boutonniere was trimmed with *Dasylirion*, which also encircled the bridesmaids' bouquets, and was used to tie the place cards on to calla lilies for the reception.

RIGHT Natalia chose to decorate an arch in the garden at the hotel where her guests were to enjoy Russian caviar and champagne. The flowers include white bougainvillea, pale pink moth orchids, and green trailing *Amaranthus*. **BELOW LEFT** The hotel interior was very minimalist, and so Natalia chose structured table arrangements of domes of roses placed in glass cubes lined with limes. Each guest was given a pink calla lily, to which their place card had been tied with bear grass. **BELOW RIGHT** Natalia's *Swan Lake* theme was highlighted in the garden, where two ice swan sculptures were floated on the central pond and surrounded by orchid heads. The guests mingled outside while listening to Tchaikovsky's *Swan Lake*.

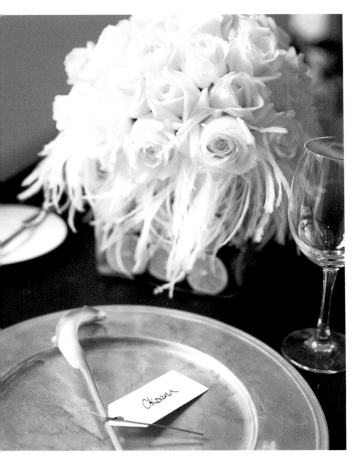

"The pale colors and the feathers added the air of a romantic fairytale – just the way I imagined my wedding!" NATALIA

how to make a centerpiece arrangement

Long tables require linear arrangements for their centers. They can often be very narrow (some are only 2 feet wide), which means that once you have got place settings on either side of the table, you have very little room for any decoration. The arrangement shown here was originally designed for a long narrow table, because it is a neat structural design and suits a narrow space perfectly. This arrangement is the width of a standard block of floral foam, called a rackette. It has a plastic base—perfect for tables. To edge the plastic and the foam you can use *Equisetum* as seen here or any other type of reed. Lavender or rosemary pinned all around the foam would work equally well, or another favorite of mine is to use cinnamon sticks for winter weddings.

The choice of flower is more limited than the choice of plant material for the surround as, for this design to look sculptural, it needs to include flower heads of a uniform size. Even if you use roses as I have done, you need to make sure that the heads are of a similar size to create the uniform bands of colour. Small germini gerberas would work well or try dahlias or zinnias. Choose vibrant colors—practically any combinations work, as long as you make sure that each variety of rose has the same depth of color. (Pastels can also work, with the use of white.) I like to take a combination and place colors that contrast with one another, to make the linear arrangement more striking.

MATERIALS

20-inch (50-cm) rackette of floral foam
A selection of long heavy stub wires
3 bunches of *Equisetum*
52 stems of roses in at least five different colors
A length of matching ribbon
Scissors

HOW TO

1 Soak the block of foam in water until the air bubbles stop rising. Bend the stub wires into two and then cut the long stems into three or four lengths, depending on the height, so that the *Equisetum* will be about 1¼ inch (2.5 cm) above the edge of the floral foam.
2 Pin the *Equisetum* into the foam, and work all the way round the block. Take care to pin the reeds in at the same height, so that this can later be concealed by the ribbon.
3 Cut a length of ribbon so that it will fit around all four sides, and tie it at one end of the block. Take another piece of ribbon, and make three loops to create a bow at one end.
4 Cut the rose heads down to about 2 inches (5 cm) of stem, so their heads sit just above the edge of the *Equisetum* and there is enough stem to take up water from the soaked foam. For the design to work, it is important that the lines of color are even. Think carefully about the order of the bands of color that will look most striking. I like to use a dark color next to a light or bright color to create the most impact. Add the roses, and mist with a water spray.

how to make an **orange basket**

Using fruit and vegetables is an inexpensive way to add more natural texture and color to your arrangements. Fruit also adds a very fresh look to arrangements, and it is perfect for a table center for a special occasion. I am drawn to fruit and vegetable markets for inspiration for my arrangements from the appearance of the soft fruits (such as red currants, strawberries, and raspberries) in early summer, to the less productive winter months when I may be on the look out for vibrant citrus fruits to add color. This arrangement was conceived with apples, and you can see an autumnal version of this on page 108. Any hard fruit, such as citrus fruits or apples, can be wired into a basket. You need a sturdy loose-weave basket to make the base and heavy stub wires to push through the center of the fruit and attach them to the basket. I prefer baskets with chicken wire in them, which makes it easier, but you can use any basket as long as there is room to push the wires through. For taller baskets I have also used vegetables. Leeks are one of my favourites; I love the root structure and the graduation of color from white to green. Turnips and heather were used for weddings with a Scottish theme, and pomegranates filled with garden roses also worked extraordinarily well. You are limited only by your imagination, so choose seasonal vegetables or fruit that can give great impact for a reasonable price. For this arrangement, I wanted to create a vibrant clash of color to complement the intense orange fruit.

MATERIALS

24 to 30 pieces of fruit
1 block of floral foam and a sturdy basket
A couple of handfuls of moss
Scissors and a selection of long strong stub wires
10 'Queensday' roses
10 stems of Icelandic poppies
10 stems of 'Pauline Burgundy' ranunculus
5 stems of *Viburnum opulus* and gardenia foliage
10 stems of huckleberry foliage
5 stems of long gloriosa lilies
7 stems of 'Milano' roses

HOW TO

1 Wire the fruit by placing a long heavy wire through the center and then bring the two ends together underneath and twist. If it is strong enough, you will be able to hold the fruit upright on the wires. If it bends, use two wires together.

2 Wire the fruit onto the basket, completing the lower ring first. Line it with moss. Add a plastic pot filled with soaked foam. The foam should be 2 inches (5 cm) above the top of the fruit.

3 Using the three foliage plants, first create the round shape of the arrangement, making sure that some of the *Viburnum opulus* falls over the edge of the basket.

4 Arrange the 'Queensday' roses at different heights and depths throughout the arrangement (but all radiating from the center). Next, add the poppies, after re-sealing the ends of their stems with a lit candle. Finally, gently guide the stems of rancunulus and gloriosa into the foam.

elegance personified

the historic setting of Syon Park, a magnificent eighteenth-century house, was the choice of wedding site for Anna and Philipp, who met while working at an investment bank. Although Philipp is from Germany and Anna from England they wanted to marry in the city where they first met. The classic wedding ceremony took place in the house itself, while the reception was held in the truly stunning Great Conservatory—I have to admit it is one of my favorite wedding sites.

After an initial visit to my studio, Anna, Philipp, and their baby daughter Sophie met me at Syon to look at the site and decide on the decorations. They chose a pale cream and white theme with a touch of pink, and decided to include some sweet peas and some tuberose for scent, and silver eucalyptus to match the rented chairs and urns. Anna and Philipp especially wanted the celebration to be perfumed, so that the wonderful fragrance would always remind them of the day. The couple chose to have low arrangements for their tables in the conservatory, as the party was quite intimate, with only 80 guests, and the site is relatively small. For the ceremony itself, Anna and Philipp chose to have two large pedestals filled with matching blooms and to line the aisle with pew ends. After the ceremony, everything had to be cleared from Syon House, as it is still a private home, and so we positioned ten of the pew ends as chairbacks around the top table and also moved the large pedestal displays to the conservatory. This was all completed discreetly while the guests enjoyed drinks and canapés in the beautiful gardens, and the informal photography was going on. Anna included some lovely personal touches to her reception by giving everyone jar of bubble mixture, which were used instead of confetti as the couple entered the reception. They also ordered a traditional red bus for transporting all their guests to Syon Park, and chose a white cab decorated with white ribbons for themselves.

ABOVE Anna and Philipp stride out together in the library of Syon House after their ceremony, in the pink with their 'Bianca Candy' roses. Anna wore a silk organza dress beaded with Swarovski crystals and a matching tiara. Philipp's gray morning suit, tie, and vest coordinate beautifully with the bridesmaids' silver silk dresses. **OPPOSITE** Two large pedestals of matching blooms are the focal point of the arrangements at the ceremony.

For the ceremony, Anna had chosen silver chairs to continue her silver color scheme, and and so we decided to use silver vases and plinths. As it turned out, the silver chairs did not make it to the ceremony (although they did arrive in time for the reception), and so we used the ones at Syon. I mention this, for to their credit, Anna and Philipp did not let this incident spoil their special day. Often when you have been planning an event for a long time and have taken time to decide on all the details and rent lots of extras to ensure that absolutely everything coordinates it can be very upsetting if things do not work exactly as planned. However, it is essential to remember that it is your special day and nothing should stop you enjoying it!

OPPOSITE This is a classic chairback, made for the top table, created by tying summer flowers and foliage into a simple swag. The peony roses are 'Scented Pink' and the classic open rose is 'Bianca Candy', which is mixed with silver *Eucalyptus* 'Baby Blue', to tone with the chair color, and pale pink snowberries (*Symphoricarpos* x *doorenbosii* 'Red Pearl'), to blend with the roses. ABOVE LEFT A bridegroom often has a different color boutoniere from those of the ushers to match the bride's bouquet, so our groom wore a pale pink 'Bianca Candy' rose trimmed with snowberries and edged with camellia leaves. The cream 'Vendela' is one of the most popular wedding roses because of its delicate color and perfect bud shape. ABOVE RIGHT The bridesmaids carry simple tied bouquets of 'Vendela' roses edged with camellia leaves. LEFT A glass bowl is a classic container for any location. The roses have been mixed with fragrant tuberose, and I used white *Lysimachia* and cream lisianthus, as they are long and create some movement. In the background a huge pedestal of flowers harmonzies with the table arrangements.

"The conservatory was more lovely and magical than anything I could ever have imagined. I loved my bouquet above anything. It was perfect and exquisite – and I had serious second thoughts about tossing it because I would have liked to keep it forever!" ANNA

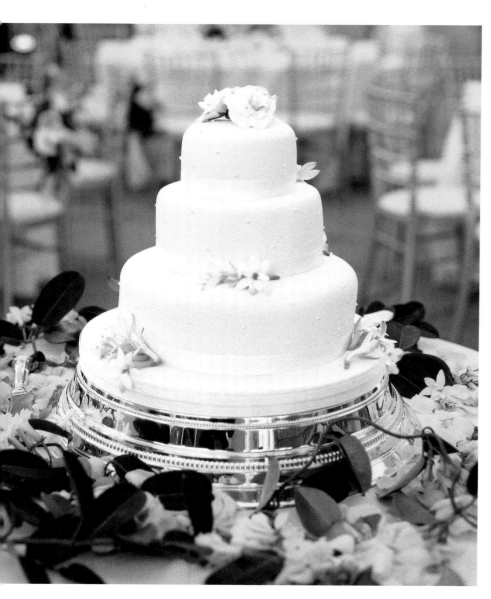

LEFT The elegant cake is set on a silver cake stand edged with fragrant stephanotis, rose petals, and votives. The cake included a few sparkly iced crystals to match Anna's shoes, dress, and tiara. **ABOVE** One of the grooms- men in front of the conservatory at Syon sporting a champagne-colored 'Vendela' rose boutonniere. **OPPOSITE, TOP LEFT** The place cards were laid out on scented garden rose petals. **OPPOSITE, TOP RIGHT** Anna chose 'Bianca Candy' roses for her bouquet to match her dress. They were wired into a deli- cate nosegay with a ribboned handle, and Philipp sported a matching boutonniere. **OPPOSITE, BOTTOM RIGHT** A tied nosegay of 'Vendela and 'Bianca Candy' roses, with white sweet peas and *Lysimachia*, edged with camellias and snowberries. **OPPOSITE, BOTTOM LEFT** Standard privet trees decorated with ribbons and roses are placed at either side of the conservatory doors to welcome guests.

floral color glossary

1 *Mimosa* 'Yellow Island' 2 *Pittosporum crassifolium* 'Variegatum' 3 *Helleborus argutifolius* 4 *Lysimachia clethroides* (white loosestrife) 5 *Genista tenera* 'Golden Shower' (broom) 6 *Tulipa* 'Weber's Parrot' 7 *Ranunculus* 'Ranobelle Donkergeel' 8 *Euphorbia fulgens* 'Quicksilver' 9 *Narcissus* 'Cheerfulness' 10 *Narcissus* 'Golden Ducat' 11 *Lathyrus odoratus* (sweet pea) 12 *Populus deltoides* (eastern cottonwood) 13 *Polianthes tuberosa* (tuberose) 14 *Euonymus fortunei* 'Emerald'n'Gold' 15 *Tulipa* 'Monte Carlo' 16 *Zantedeschia* 'Florex Gold' (arum lily, calla lily) 17 *Rosa* 'Taxi' 18 *Spiraea nipponica* 'Snowmound' 19 *Antirrhinum majus* 'Winter Euro Yellow' (snapdragon) 20 *Gerbera germini* 'Kaliki' 21 *Viburnum opulus* (guelder rose) 22 *Abutilon vitifolium* var. *album* 23 *Eustoma grandiflorum* 'Piccolo Yellow' (lisianthus) 24 *Polygonatum* (Solomon's seal) 25 *Forsythia* x *intermedia* 26 *Prunus glandulosa* 'Albo Plena'

1 *Eucalyptus ficifolia* 2 *Rosa* 'Aqua' 3 *Camellia* x *williamsii* 'E.G. Waterhouse' 4 *Rosa* 'Milano' 5 *Anemone coronaria* 'Mona Lisa Pink' 6 *Tulipa* 'Upstar' 7 *Lathyrus odoratus* (sweet pea) 8 *Tulipa* 'Lucky Strike' 9 *Hyacinthus orientalis* 'Anna Marie' (hyacinth) 10 *Paeonia* 'Sarah Bernhardt' 11 *Paeonia* 'Bowl of Beauty' 12 *Eustoma grandiflorum* 'Moon Pink' (lisianthus) 13 *Chamelaucium uncinatum* 'Wendy Rose' (Geralton wax) 14 *Phlox* 'Bright Eyes' 15 *Rosa* 'Laminuette' 16 *Tulipa* 'Salmon Parrot' 17 *Gerbera germini* 'Sonate' 18 *Chaenomeles japonica* (flowering quince) 19 *Gladiolus* 'Priscilla' 20 *Prunus serrulata* 21 *Ranunculus* 'Ranobelle Inra dark pink' 22 *Ranunculus* 'Ranobelle Inra light pink' 23 *Antirrhinum majus* 'Potomac Red' (snapdragon)

1 *Delphinium* 'Skyline' 2 *Agapanthus* 'Donau' 3 *Consolida ajacis* 'Sydney Purple' (larkspur) 4 *Delphinium* Belladonna Group 'Völkerfrieden' 5 *Liatris spicata* 'Blue Bird' (gayfeather) 6 *Veronica longifolia* 'Blauriesen' 7 *Delphinium* Belladonna Group 'Sky Lady' 8 *Freesia* 'Côte d'Azur' 9 *Matthiola incana* 'Arabella' (stock) 10 *Tulipa* 'Black Parrot' 11 *Iris* 'Purple Rain' 12 *Lathyrus odoratus* (sweet pea) 13 *Aquilegia* 'Blue Lady' (columbine) 14 *Scilla siberica* (Siberian squill) 15 *Myosotis sylvatica* (forget-me-not) 16 *Hyacinthus orientalis* 'Delft Blue' (hyacinth) 17 *Muscari armeniacum* 'Blue Dream' (grape hyancinth) 18 *Anemone coronaria* 'Galil Purper' 19 *Anemone coronaria* 'Marianne Blue' 20 *Matthiola incana* 'Lucinda Purple' (stock) 21 *Syringa* x *hyacinthiflora* 'Esther Staley' (lilac) 22 *Trachelium caeruleum* 'Blue Wonder' (blue throatwort) 23 *Syringa vulgaris* 'Andenken an Ludwig Spaeth' (lilac)

1 *Viburnum opulus* (guelder rose) 2 *Dahlia* 'Bicolour Karma' 3 *Rosa* 'Extase' 4 *Rosa* 'Jacaranda' 5 *Dianthus barbatus* 'Monarch Series' (sweet William) 6 *Gerbera* 'Dark Serena' 7 *Cirsium japonicum* 'Pink Beauty' 8 *Celosia argentea* var. *cristata* Cristata Group 'Bombay Pink' (cockscomb) 9 *Moluccella laevis* (bells of Ireland) 10 *Consolida ajacis* 'Sydney Rose' (larkspur) 11 *Paeonia lactiflora* 'Karl Rosenfield' 12 *Sorbus aria* 'Lutescens' (whitebeam) 13 *Lathyrus odoratus* (sweetpea) 14 *Rosa* 'Milano' 15 *Astilbe* x *arendsii* 'Erika' 16 *Eustoma grandiflorum* 'Mariachi Pink' (lisianthus) 17 *Rosa* 'Saint Celia' 18 *Crataegus laevigata* 'Paul's Scarlet' (may, hawthorn) 19 *Protea nerifolia* 20 *Lilium* 'Red Sox' 21 *Celosia argentea* var. *cristata* Plumosa Group 'Bombay Fire'

1 *Physalis alkekengi* (Chinese lantern) 2 *Populus deltoides* (eastern cottonwood) 3 *Crocosmia* 'Lucifer' (montbretia)
4 *Chrysanthemum* 'Salmon Fairie' 5 *Leucospermum reflexum* 'Lutea' (pincushion) 6 *Helenium* 'Moerheim Beauty' 7 *Zantedeschia*
'Florex Gold' (arum lily, calla lily) 8 *Capsicum annuum* 9 *Carthamus tinctorius* 'Kinko' (safflower, false saffron) 10 *Anethum*
graveolens (dill) 11 *Hydrangea macrophylla* 12 *Rosa* 'Golden Gate' 13 *Helianthus annuus* 'Sonja' (sunflower) 14 *Hypericum* 'Jade
Flair' (St. John's Wort) 15 *Chrysanthemum* 'Shamrock' 16 *Sandersonia aurantiaca* 17 *Malus* x *robusta* 'Red Sentinel' (crab apple)

1 *Gentiana* 'Sky' (gentian) 2 *Delphinium* Belladonna Group 'Blue Shadow' 3 *Rosa* 'Blue Moon' 4 *Ageratum houstonianum* 'Blue Horizon' 5 *Centaurea montana* (knapweed) 6 *Scabiosa stellata* 'Ping Pong' (pincushion flower, scabious) 7 *Lathyrus odoratus* 'Lila' (sweet pea) 8 *Cotinus coggygria* 'Royal Purple' (smoke bush) 9 *Zantedeschia* 'Anneke' (arum lily, calla lily) 10 *Delphinium* 'Faust' 11 *Allium sphaerocephalon* 12 *Delphinium* 'Lilac Arrow' 13 *Hydrangea macrophylla* 'Blue' 14 *Scabiosa caucasica* 'Clive Greaves' (pincushion flower, scabious) 15 *Rosa* 'Blue Gene' 16 *Delphinium* 'Skyline'

1 *Symphoricarpos* x *doorenbosii* 'White Hedge' (snowberry) 2 *Astilbe* 'America' 3 *Symphoricarpos* 'Pink Pearl' (snowberry)
4 *Panicum miliaceum* (millet) 5 *Gerbera germini* 'Leila' 6 *Bouvardia* 'Bridesmaid' 7 *Rosa* 'Jacaranda' 8 *Rosa* 'Aqua' 9 *Rosa*
'Duo Unique' 10 *Sedum telephium* 'Mohrchen' 11 *Cirsium japonicum* 'Pink Beauty' 12 *Rosa* 'Mimi Eden' 13 *Rosa* 'Illusion'
14 *Celosia argentea* var. *cristata* Cristata Group'Bombay Rose' 15 *Alchemilla mollis* (lady's mantle) 16 *Dahlia* 'Karma Thalia'
17 *Zantedeschia* 'Fantail Candy' (arum lily, calla lily)

1 *Rosa* 'Bianca' 2 *Lathyrus odoratus* (sweet pea) 3 *Celosia argentea* var. *cristata* Cristata Group 'Bombay Green' (cockscomb)
4 *Dahlia* 'Canberra' 5 *Dianthus* 'Prado' (pink) 6 *Gypsophila* 'Million Stars' 7 *Lysimachia clethroides* 'Helene' (loosestrife)
8 *Trachelium caeruleum* 'Album' (throatwort) 9 *Rosa virginiana* 10 *Scabiosa caucasica* 'Hermina' (pincushion flower, scabious)
11 *Anthemis tinctoria* (golden marguerite, oxeye chamomile) 12 *Symphoricarpos albus* 'White Pearl' (snowberry)

1 *Ilex aquifolium* 'Golden Verboon' (common holly) 2 *Solanum integrifolium* (tomato eggplant) 3 *Fagus sylvatica* (beech)
4 *Leucospermum cordifolium* 'Tango' (pincushion) 5 *Dendrobium* 'Tang' 6 *Ranunculus* 'Ranobelle Inra Oranjerood'
7 *Quercus robur* (English oak, common oak) 8 *Zantedeschia* 'Treasure' (arum lily, calla lily) 9 *Eucalyptus pulverulenta*
10 *Rosa* 'Macarena' 11 *Chrysanthemum* 'Reagan Orange' 12 *Euphorbia fulgens* 'Beatrix' 13 *Gladiolus* 'Esta Bonita'
14 *Chrysanthemum* 'Tom Pearce' 15 *Hippeastrum* 'Rilona' (amaryllis) 16 *Quercus palustris* (pin oak) 17 *Tulipa* 'Prinses Irene'

1 *Gladiolus* 'Addi' 2 *Capsicum annum* (pepper) 3 *Anemone* 'Mona Lisa Red' 4 *Rosa canina* (dog rose, common brier)
5 *Hippeastrum* 'Red Lion' (amaryllis) 6 *Photinia* x *fraseri* 'Red Robin' 7 *Ilex verticillata* 'Oosterwijk' (winterberry)
8 *Gerbera germini* 'Salsa' 9 *Rosa* 'Grand Prix' 10 *Callistemon citrinus* (crimson bottlebrush) 11 *Chrysanthemum* 'Reagan
Red' 12 *Skimmia japonica* 'Rubella' 13 *Leucadendron* 'Safari Sunset' 14 *Chrysanthemum* 'Early Bird Red' 15 *Tulipa*
'Prominence' 16 *Anthurium* 'Choco' (flamingo flower) 17 *Rosa* 'Black Baccara' 18 *Ranunculus* 'Pauline Scarlet'
19 *Gerbera germini* 'Midnight' 20 *Alpinia purpurata* (red ginger)

1 *Hippeastrum* 'Ludwig Dazzler' (amaryllis) 2 *Euphorbia fulgens* 'Largo White' 3 *Rosa* 'Avalanche' 4 *Brassica oleracea* 'Corgy White' (ornamental cabbage) 5 *Chamelaucium uncinatum* 'Blondie' (Geraldton wax) 6 *Lilium longiflorum* 'White Europe' (Easter lily) 7 *Brunia albiflora* 8 *Dahlia* 'Karma Serena' 9 *Gladiolus* 'Mont Blanc' 10 *Gossypium herbaceum* (levant cotton) 11 *Genista* 12 *Eucharis amazonica* 13 *Syringa vulgaris* 'Primrose' (lilac) 14 *Hyacinthus orientalis* 'Mont Blanc' (hyacinth) 15 *Ranunculus* 'Ranobelle Inra White' 16 *Narcissus tazetta* 'Ziva' 17 *Lilum* 'Casa Blanca' 18 *Phalaenopsis* 'Alpha' 19 *Gypsophila* 'Lucky Stars' 20 *Hydrangea arborescens* 'Annabelle' 21 *Anthurium* 'Bianca'

1 *Zantedeschia aethiopica* 'Colombe de la Paix' (arum lily, calla lily) 2 *Eucharis amazonica* 3 *Brachyglottis* 'Sunshine' (senecio) 4 *Aster novi-belgii* 'M. C. Snowy' (Michaelmas daisy) 5 *Chrysanthemum* 'Reagan White' 6 *Eustoma grandiflorum* 'Alice White' (lisianthus) 7 *Freesia* 'Alaska' 8 *Ornithogalum thyrsoides* 'Mount Fuji' (chincherinchee) 9 *Hypericum androsaemum* 'King Flair' (tutsan) 10 *Rosmarinus officinalis* (rosemary) 11 *Dendrobium* 'Madame Pompadour White' 12 *Rosa* 'Iceberg' 13 *Rosa* 'Akito' 14 *Gerbera jamesonii* 'Bianca' (Barbarton daisy) 15 *Lilium longiflorum* 'Snow Queen' (Easter lily) 16 *Stephanotis floribunda* (bridal wreath, Madagascar jasmine) 17 *Cymbidium* 'R. B. Mieke' 18 *Anthurium* 'Captain' 19 *Dianthus* 'Dover' (carnation) 20 *Gypsophila* 'Little White'

index

acknowledgments

author Firstly this book would not have been possible without the wonderful brides and grooms who allowed us to share in their special day. Thanks to you all, past and present, over the last fifteen years and to the following brides whose weddings have been shown in this book: Claire Bailey, Shelly-Ann Bowdler, Natalie Chamberlain, Naomi Cuthbert, Anna Dalton-Knott, Monica Gillett, Julie Harper, Jane Houghton, Natalia Kudimova, Penny Mallinson, Sarah Miller, Annabel Pincus, Bella Pringle, Jenny Reid, Karen Sear, Keren Spier.

Thank you to all the featured venues: The Carlton Towers Hotel, London SW1; Claridges, London W1; Coq D'Argent, London EC2; Eltham Palace, Kent; Fredericks Restaurant, London N1; The Hempel Hotel, London W2; Le Manoir aux Quat' Saisons, Oxfordshire; Anton Mosimann and everyone at Mosimanns Club, London SW1; The Naval and Military Club, London SW1; The Orangery, London W11; Pallazo Pisani in Venice, Italy; The Royal Air Force Club, London W1; The Royal Geographic Society London SW7; The Savoy Hotel, London WC2; Six Hamilton Place, London W1; Syon House and Conservatory, London TW8

Thank you to all the party planners, wedding organisers, caterers and banqueting staff we have had the pleasure of working with over the years – in particular Lionel Benjamin and all at the Savoy; Joseph Cote and the team at Claridges; Peter Prescott at Conran Restaurants; and the Carlton Towers Hotel. Thank you to all the caterers we have worked with in this book; Jalpeno who organised the wedding at Syon House and Rochelle Sassoon who organised Keren and Dani Spier's wedding. Thanks also to Bluebird 2 You, London SW3; Tony Page, London NW10; Carole Sobell, London NW9; and Kate Pouler of Pat-A-Cake (020 7485 0006) and Mich Turner at the Little Venice Cake Company (020 7486 5252) for their help with the cake section. Thank you also to the wedding organisers including Sophie Lillingstone (020 7384 0684) for her help with Monica Gillett's wedding.

A huge thank you to Karen Pocock and all at the Wedding Shop both in the Fulham Road and at Liberty for all their assistance. Also to Vera Wang for creating the dresses that made so many of the brides featured in this book look perfect on their wedding day. A special thanks to the staff at the Wedding Shop at Liberty for the feature on pages 48–9 of the gorgeous Vera Wang dresses. Thank you also to Jacques Azagury; Christina Couture; Ritva Westinus.

It was my great pleasure to work with Chris Tubbs, who so calmly and beautifully photographed many of our weddings and added his creativity to the still-life photographs. An enormous thank you to Valerie Fong, my art director, who kept us on track and gave her all to this project and has been responsible for making it into this stunningly beautiful book. Thank you also to Valerie for her good humour and patience throughout! Thanks to Emma Callery who started off as my editor, for her input, and an enormous thanks to Vicki Vrint who picked up the project halfway through and managed to get me to meet the deadline in the most professional and enduring manner! Thanks for all your hard work and for all the people behind the scenes who have worked on the production – in particular Geoff Barlow. Thank you to the Paula Pryke team who have been very supportive throughout the making of this book – in particular to Samantha Griffiths, Ashleigh Hopkins, Sarah Jackson, Julie Redden – and to all our wonderful suppliers, especially Dennis Edwards and all the hard-working growers. It has also been my pleasure to work with Pascal Plessis and all the photographers at Contre-Jour (see right) who provided photographs of weddings that we worked on together over the years.

Finally thanks to my bridegroom Peter for his love and support and for sixteen wonderful years together!

All photographs are by Chris Tubbs except for those taken by:
Paula Pryke – p93 top & far right
Contre-Jour, 40 Martell Road, London, SE21 4EN (020 8670 1234) – p13 all; p14 bottom right; p36-7 all; p45 top left; p46 all; p47 bottom; p51 top left; p70-73 all; p88; p91 top left & bottom; p92 all; p93 bottom left & bottom right; p99; p107 top right; p109 bottom